# Essays - Classical

# E S S A Y S

## CLASSICAL

BY

F. W. H. MYERS

London
MACMILLAN AND CO., Limited
NEW YORK: THE MACMILLAN COMPANY
1904

*First printed (Crown 8vo)* 1883
*Reprinted* 1888.   *Reprinted (Globe 8vo)* 1897, 1901, 1904

# PREFATORY NOTE.

In reprinting this Essay from *Hellenica*, I have
thought it needless to repeat my original list of
authorities consulted. Since the Essay was written
M. Bouché-Leclercq has published his *Histoire de
la Divination dans l'Antiquité*, where the biblio-
graphy of the subject is given with exhaustive
fulness. The chief resources to oracles in classical
authors have been long ago collected, and are now
the common property of scholars. The last considerable addition to the list was made by G. Wolff,
and they have been judiciously arranged by Maury
and others. What is needed is a true comprehension
of them, towards which less progress has been
made than the ordinary reader may suppose. Even
Bouché-Leclercq, whose accuracy and completeness
within his self-proposed limits deserve high admiration, expressly excludes from his purview the lessons
and methods of comparative ethnology, and hardly

cares to consider what those phenomena in reality *were* whose history he is recounting. I can claim little more of insight into their true nature than suffices to make me conscious of ignorance, but I have at least tried to indicate where the problems lie, and in what general directions we must look for their solution.

It is indeed true (as was remarked by several critics when this Essay first appeared) that I have kept but inadequately my implied promise of illustrating ancient mysteries by the light of modern discovery. But my difficulty lay not in the defect but in the excess of parallelism between ancient and modern phenomena. I found that each explicit reference of this kind would raise so many questions that the sequence of the narrative would soon have been destroyed. I was obliged, therefore, to content myself with suggestions and allusions — allusions necessarily obscure to the general reader in the absence of any satisfactory treatise on similar phenomena to which he could be referred. I am not without hope that this blank may before long be filled up by a research conducted on a wider and sounder basis than heretofore; and, should the sway of recognised law extend itself farther over that shadowy land, I shall be well content if this Essay

shall be thought to have aimed, however imperfectly, at that "true interrogation" which is "the
half of science."

## POSTSCRIPT, 1887.

Since the above words were written in 1883,
some beginning of the suggested inquiries has been
recorded in the *Proceedings* of the Society for
Psychical Research. Some discussions on human
automatism which will there be found are not
without bearing on the subject of the present essay.

## POSTSCRIPT, 1897.

The work of the Society for Psychical Research
has now been pushed much further; and its
*Proceedings* (Kegan Paul, Trench, Trübner & Co.)
are indispensable for persons interested in the
inquiries above referred to.

# CONTENTS.

# GREEK ORACLES.

Οὐ μέν πως νῦν ἔστιν ἀπὸ δρυὸς οὐδ' ἀπὸ πέτρης
τῷ ὀαριζέμεναι, ἅ τε παρθένος ἠΐθεός τε,
παρθένος ἠΐθεός τ' ὀαρίζετον ἀλλήλοιιν.

## I.

IT is not only in the domain of physical inquiry that the advance of knowledge is self-accelerated at every step, and the very excellence of any given work insures its own speedier supersession. All those studies which bear upon the past of mankind are every year more fully satisfying this test of the genuinely scientific character of the plan on which they are pursued. The old conception of the world's history as a collection of stories, each admitting of a complete and definitive recital, is giving way to a conception which would compare it rather with a series of imperfectly-read inscriptions, the sense of each of which is modified by the interpretations which we gradually find for its predecessors.

And of no department is this truer than of the comparative history of religions. The very idea of such a study is of recent growth, and no sooner is the attempt made to colligate by general laws the enormous mass of the religious phenomena of the world than we find that the growing science is in danger of being choked by its own luxuriance—that each conflicting hypothesis in turn seems to draw superabundant proof from the myriad beliefs and practices of men. We may, indeed, smile at the extravagances of one-sided upholders of each successive system. We need not believe with Bishop Huet[1] that Moses was the archetype both of Adonis and of Priapus. Nor, on the other hand, need we suppose with Pierson[2] that Abraham himself was originally a stone god. We may leave Dozy[3] to pursue his own conjecture, and deduce the strange story of the Hebrew race from their worship of the planet Saturn. Nor need the authority of Anonymus *de Rebus Incredibilibus*[4] constrain us to accept his view that Paris was a young man who wrote essays on goddesses, and Phaethon an unsuccessful astronomer.

But it is far from easy to determine the relative validity of the theories of which these are exaggerated expressions,—to decide (for instance) what place is to be given to the direct transference of

[1] *Demonstr. Evang.* iii. 3, viii. 5.
[2] Ap. Kuenen, *Religion of Israel*, i 390.
[3] *Ibid.* i. 262.
[4] *Opuscula Mythologica* (Amst. 1688).

beliefs from nation to nation, to fetish-worship, to
the worship of the heavenly bodies, to the deification
of dead men.   In an essay like the present, dealing
only with a fragment of this great inquiry, it will
be safest to take the most general view, and to say
that man's fear and wonder invest every object, real
or imaginary, which strongly impresses him,——beasts
or stones, or souls and spirits, or fire and the sun in
heaven,——with an intelligence and a power darkly
resembling his own ; and, moreover, that certain
phenomena, real or supposed,——dreams and epilepsy,
eclipse and thunder, sorceries and the uprising of
the dead,——recur from time to time to supply him
with apparent proof of the validity of his beliefs,
and to modify those beliefs according to the nature
of his country and his daily life.   Equally natural
is it that, as his social instincts develop and his
power of generalisation begins, he will form such
conceptions as those of a moral government of the
world, of a retributory hereafter, of a single Power
from which all others emanate, or into which they
disappear.

   Avoiding, therefore, any attempt to take a side
among conflicting theories, I will draw from the
considerations which follow no further moral than
one which is well-nigh a truism, though too often
forgotten in the heat of debate, namely, that we are
assuredly not as yet in a position to pass a final
judgment on the forms which religion has assumed

in the past; we have traversed too small a part of
the curve of human progress to determine its true
character; even yet, in fact, "we are ancients of the
earth, and in the morning of the times." The difficulty of bearing this clearly in mind, great in every
age, becomes greater as each age advances more
rapidly in knowledge and critical power. In this
respect the eighteenth century teaches us an obvious
lesson. That century witnessed a marked rise in
the standard of historical evidence, a marked enlightenment in dealing with the falsities and superstitions of the past. The consequence was that all
things seemed explicable; that whatever could not
be reduced to ordinary rules seemed only worthy of
being brushed aside. Since that day the standard
of evidence in history has not declined,—it has
become stricter still; but at the same time the
need of sympathy and insight, if we would comprehend the past, has become strongly felt, and has
modified or suspended countless judgments which
the philosophers of the last century delivered without misgiving. The difference between the two
great critics and philosophers of France, at that day
and in our own, shows at a glance the whole gulf
between the two points of view. How little could
the readers of Voltaire have anticipated Renan!
How little could they have imagined that their
master's trenchant arguments would so soon have
fallen to the level of half-educated classes and half-

civilised nations,—would have been formidable only
in sixpenny editions, or when translated into Hindo-
stani for the confutation of missionary zeal!

What philosophical enlightenment was in the
last century, science, physical or historical, is in our
own.   Science is the power to which we make our
first and undoubting appeal, and we run a corresponding risk of assuming that she can already solve
problems wholly, which as yet she can solve only in
part,—of adopting under her supposed guidance
explanations which may hereafter be seen to have
the crudity and one-sidedness of Voltaire's treatment
of Biblical history.

The old school of theologians were apt to assume
that because all men—or all men whom they chose
to count—had held a certain belief, that belief must
be true.   Our danger lies rather in being too ready
to take for granted that when we have explained
how a belief arose we have done with it altogether;
that because a tenet is of savage parentage it hardly
needs formal disproof.   In this view the wide diffusion of a belief serves only to stamp its connection
with uncivilised thought, and " quod semper, quod
ubique, quod ab omnibus," has become to many
minds rather the badge of superstition than the test
of catholic truth.   That any one but ourselves should
have held a creed seems to lower the average intelligence of its adherents.

Yet, on behalf of savages, and our ancestors in

general), there may be room for some apology. If we reflect how large a part of human knowledge consists of human emotion, we may even say that they possessed some forms of knowledge which we have since lost. The mind of man (it has been well said), like the earth on which he walks, undergoes perpetual processes of denudation as well as of deposit. We ourselves, as children, did in a sense know much which we know no more; our picture of the universe, incomplete and erroneous as it was, wore some true colours which we cannot now recall. The child's vivid sensibility, reflected in his vivifying imagination, is as veritably an inlet of truth as if it were an added clearness of physical vision; and though the child himself has not judgment enough to use his sensibilities aright, yet if the man is to discern the poetic truth about Nature, he will need to recall to memory his impressions as a child.

Now, in this way too, the savage is a kind of child; his beliefs are not always to be summarily referred to his ignorance; there may be something in them which we must realise in imagination before we venture to explain it away. Ethnologists have recognised the need of this difficult self-identification with the remote past, and have sometimes remarked, with a kind of envy, how much nearer the poet is than the philosopher to the savage habit of mind.

There is, however, one ancient people in whose case much of this difficulty disappears, whose re-

ligion may be traced backwards through many
phases into primitive forms, while yet it is easy to
study its records with a fellow-feeling which grows
with our knowledge till it may approach almost to
an identity of spirit.   Such is the ascendency which
the great works of the Greek imagination have established over the mind of man, that it is no paradox
to say that the student's danger lies often in excess
rather than in defect of sympathy.   He is tempted
to ignore the real superiority of our own religion,
morality, civilisation, and to re-shape in fancy an
adult world on an adolescent ideal.   But the remedy
for over-estimates, as well as for under-estimates,
lies in an increased definiteness of knowledge, an
ever-clearer perception of the exact place in the
chain of development which Greek thought and
worship hold.   The whole story of Greek mythology
must ere long be retold in a form as deeply modified
by comparative ethnology as our existing treatises
have been modified by comparative philology.   Such
a task would be beyond my powers; but while
awaiting some more comprehensive treatment of the
subject by a better-qualified hand, I have in this
Essay endeavoured to trace,—by suggestion rather
than in detail, but with constant reference to the
results of recent science, — the development and
career in Greece of one remarkable class of religious
phenomena which admits to some extent of separate
treatment.

Greek oracles reflect for a thousand years [1] the spiritual needs of a great people. They draw their origin from an Animism [2] which almost all races share, and in their early and inarticulate forms they contain a record of most of the main currents in which primitive beliefs are wont to run. Afterwards—closely connected both with the idea of supernatural possession and with the name of the sun-god Apollo—they exhibit a singular fusion of nature-worship with Shahmanism or sorcery. Then, as the non-moral and naturalistic conception of the deity yields to the moral conception of him as an idealised man, the oracles reflect the change, and the Delphian god becomes in a certain sense the conscience of Greece.

A period of decline follows; due, as it would seem, partly to the depopulation and political ruin of Greece, but partly also to the indifference or scepticism of her dominant schools of philosophy. But this decline is followed by a revival which forms one of the most singular of those apparent checks which complicate the onward movement of thought by ever new modifications of the beliefs of the remote past. So far as this complex movement

[1] Roughly speaking, from 700 B.C. to 300 A.D., but the earliest oracles probably date much farther back.

[2] It is hardly necessary to say that by Animism is meant a belief in the existence around us of souls or spirits, whether disembodied, as ghosts, or embodied in fetishes, animals, etc. Shahmanism is a word derived from the title of the Siberian wizards, who procure by agitated trance some manifestation from their gods.

can be at present understood, it seems to have been connected among the mass of the people with the wide-spread religious upheaval of the first Christian centuries, and to have been at last put an end to by Christian baptism or sword. Among the higher minds it seems to have rested partly on a perplexed admission of certain phenomena, partly on the strongly-felt need of a permanent and elevated revelation, which yet should draw its origin from the Hellenic rather than the Hebrew past. And the story reaches a typical conclusion in the ultimate disengagement of the highest natures of declining Greece from mythology and ceremonial, and the absorption of definite dogma into an overwhelming ecstasy.

## II.

The attempt to define the word "oracle" confronts us at once with the difficulties of the subject. The Latin term, indeed, which we are forced to employ, points specially to cases where the voice of God or spirit was actually heard, whether directly or through some human intermediary. But the corresponding Greek term (μαντεῖον) merely signifies a seat of soothsaying, a place where divinations are obtained by whatever means. And we must not regard the oracles of Greece as rare and majestic phenomena, shrines founded by a full-grown mythology for the direct habitation of a god. Rather they are the products of a long process of evolution, the modified survivals from among countless holy places of a primitive race.

Greek literature has preserved to us abundant traces of the various causes which led to the ascription of sanctity to some particular locality. Oftenest it is some chasm or cleft in the ground, filled, perhaps, with mephitic vapours, or with the mist of a subterranean stream, or merely opening in its dark obscurity an inlet into the mysteries of the underworld. Such was the chasm of the Clarian,[1] the Delian,[2] the Delphian Apollo; and such the oracle of the prophesying nymphs on Cithæron.[3] Such was Trophonius' cave,[4] and his own name perhaps is only a synonym for the Mother Earth, "in many names the one identity," who nourishes at once and reveals.[5]

Sometimes—as for instance at Megara,[6] Sicyon, Orchomenus, Laodicea—the sanctity gathers around some βαίτυλος or fetish-stone, fashioned, it may be,

---

[1] Iambl. *de Myst.* p. 74.

[2] Lebègue, *Recherches sur Délos*, p. 89.

[3] Paus. ix. 3. See also Paus. v. 14, for a legend of an oracle of Earth herself at Olympia.

[4] Paus. ix. 39.

[5] Τροφώνιος from τρέφω. The visitor, who lay a long time, οὐ μάλα συμφρονῶν ἐναργῶς εἴτ᾽ ἐγρήγορεν εἴτ᾽ ὠνειροπόλει (Plut. *de Genio Socratis*, 22), had doubtless been partially asphyxiated. St. Patrick's Purgatory was perhaps conducted on the same plan.

[6] Paus. i. 43, and for further references on bætyls see Lebègue, p. 85. See also Lubbock, *Origin of Civilisation*, p. 225.

into a column or pyramid, and probably in most
cases identified at first with the god himself, though,
after the invention of statuary, its significance might
be obscured or forgotten.   Such stones outlast all
religions, and remain for us in their rude shapeless-
ness the oldest memorial of the aspirations or the
fears of man.

Sometimes the sacred place was merely some
favourite post of observation of the flight of birds,
or of lightning, like Teiresias' "ancient seat of
augury,"[1] or the hearth[2] from which, before the
sacred embassy might start for Delphi, the Pythaists
watched above the crest of Parnes for the summons
of the heavenly flame.

Or it might be merely some spot where the
divination from burnt-offerings seemed unusually
true and plain,—at Olympia, for instance, where, as
Pindar tells us, "soothsayers divining from sacrifice
make trial of Zeus who lightens clear."   It is needless to speak at length of groves and streams and
mountain-summits, which in every region of the
world have seemed to bring the unseen close to man
by waving mystery, or by rushing murmur, or by
nearness to the height of heaven.[3]   It is enough to

---

[1] Soph. *Ant.* 1001 ; Paus. ix. 16 ; and cf. Eur. *Phoen.* 841.

[2] Strabo, ix. p. 619.  They watched ἀπὸ τῆς ἐσχάρας τοῦ ἀστραπαίου
Διός.  See also Eur. *Ion.* 295.  Even a place where lots were custom-
arily drawn might become a seat of oracle.—Paus. vii. 25.

[3] There is little trace in Greece of "weather-oracles,"— such as
the Blocksberg,—hills deriving a prophetic reputation from the

understand that in Greece, as in other countries over which successive waves of immigration have passed, the sacred places were for the most part selected for primitive reasons, and in primitive times; then as more civilised races succeeded and Apollo came,— whence or in what guise cannot here be discussed, —the old shrines were dedicated to new divinities, the old symbols were metamorphosed or disappeared. The fetish-stones were crowned by statues, or replaced by statues and buried in the earth.[1] The Sibyls died in the temples, and the sun-god's island holds the sepulchre of the moon-maidens of the northern sky.[2]

It is impossible to arrange in quite logical order phenomena which touch each other at so many points, but in making our transition from these impersonal or hardly personal oracles of divination to the "voice-oracles"[3] of classical times, we may

indications of coming rain, etc., drawn from clouds on their summits. The sanctity of Olympus, as is well known, is connected with a supposed elevation above all elemental disturbances.

[1] Pind. *Ol.* viii. 3, and for further references see Hermann, *Griech. Ant.* ii. 247. Maury (ii. 447) seems to deny this localisation on insufficient grounds.

[2] The Hyperboreæ, see reff. ap. Lebègue, p. 69. M. Bouché-Leclercq's discussion (vol. ii.) of the Sibylline legends is more satisfactory than that of Klausen (*Aeneas und die Penaten*, p. 107, foll.) He describes the Sibylline type as "une personnification gracieuse de la mantique intuitive, intermédiaire entre le babil inconscient de la nymphe Écho et la sagacité inhumaine de la Sphinx."

[3] Χρησμοὶ φθεγματικοί.

first mention the well-known Voice or Rumour which as early as Homer runs heaven-sent through the multitude of men, or sometimes prompts to revolution by "the word of Zeus."[1]

To this we may add the belief that words spoken at some critical and culminant, or even at some arbitrarily-chosen moment, have a divine significance. We find some trace of this in the oracle of Teiresias,[2] and it appears in a strange form in an old oracle said to have been given to Homer, which tells him to beware of the moment when some young children shall ask him a riddle which he is unable to answer.[3] Cases of omens given by a chance word in classical times are too familiar to need further reference.[4] What we have to notice here is, that this casual method of learning the will of heaven was systematised into a practice at certain oracular temples, where the applicant made his sacrifice, stopped his ears, went into the market-place, and accepted the first words

[1] ὄσσα, φήμη, κληδών, ὀμφή—Il. ii. 93; Herod. ix. 100 ; Od. iii. 215, etc. These words are probably used sometimes for regular oracular communications.

[2] Od. xi. 126.

[3] ἀλλὰ νέων παίδων αἴνιγμα φύλαξαι. Paus. x. 24; Anth. Pal. xiv. 66. This conundrum, when it was at length put to Homer, was of so vulgar a character that no real discredit is reflected on the Father of Poetry by his perplexity as to its solution. (Homeri et Hesiodi certamen, ad fin.) Heraclitus, however, used the fact to illustrate the limitation of even the highest human powers.

[4] Herodotus ix. 91, may be selected as an example of a happy chance in forcing an omen.

he happened to hear as a divine intimation.  We
hear of oracles on this pattern at Memphis,[1] and at
Pharæ in Achæa.[2]

From these voices, which, though clearly audible,
are, as it were, unowned and impersonal, we may
pass to voices which have a distinct personality,
but are heard only by the sleeping ear.  Dreams
of departed friends are likely to be the first phenomenon which inspires mankind with the idea that
they can hold converse with a spiritual world.  We
find dreams at the very threshold of the theology of
almost all nations, and accordingly it does not
surprise us to find Homer asserting that dreams
come from Zeus,[3] or painting, with a pathos which
later literature has never surpassed, the strange
vividness and agonising insufficiency of these fugi-
tive visions of the night.[4]

And throughout Greek literature presaging
dreams which form, as Plutarch says, "an unfixed
and wandering oracle of Night and Moon"[5] are

[1] Dio Chrys. ad Alex. 32, 13, παῖδες ἀπαγγέλλουσι παίζοντες τὸ δοκοῦν τῷ θεῷ.

[2] Paus. vii. 22.

[3] Il. i. 63. Or from Hermes, or earth, or the gods below.

[4] Il. xxiii. 97. If we accept the theory of an older Achilleid we find the importance of augury proper decreasing, of dreams in-creasing, in the Homeric poems themselves. Geddes, Hom. Probl. p. 186; cf. Mure, Hist. Gr. Lit. i. 492. Similarly Apollo's darts grow more gentle, and his visitations more benign.—Geddes, p. 140.

[5] Plut. Ser. Num. Vind. 22.

I.]           GREEK ORACLES.          15

abundant in every form, from the high behest laid on Bellerophon " when in the dark of night stood by him the shadowy-shielded maid, and from a dream, suddenly, a waking vision she became,"[1] down to the dreams in the temples of Serapis or of Aesculapius which Aristides the Rhetorician has embalmed for us in his Sacred Orations,—the dream which " seemed to indicate a bath, yet not without a certain ambiguity," or the dream which left him in distressing uncertainty whether he were to take an emetic or no.[2]

And just as we have seen that the custom of observing birds, or of noting the omens of casual speech, tended to fix itself permanently in certain shrines, so also dream-oracles, or temples where the inquirer slept in the hope of obtaining an answer from the god seen in vision, or from some other vision sent by him, were one of the oldest forms of oracular seats. Brizo, a dream-prophetess, preceded Apollo at Delos.[3] A similar legend contrasts "the divination of darkness" at Delphi with Apollo's clear prophetic song.[4] Night herself was believed to send visions at Megara,[5] and coins of Commodus still show us her erect and shrouded figure, the torches that glimmer in her shade. Amphiaraus,[6] Amphilo-

---

[1] Pind. *Ol.* xiii. 100.

[2] Ar. Rhet. vol. i. p. 275 (Dind.), ἔχον μέν τινα ἔννοιαν λούτρου, οὐ μέντοι χωρὶς γε ὑπονοίας, and i. 285.

[3] Athen. viii. 2, and see Lebègue, p. 218; comp. Aesch. *Ag.* 275.

[4] Eur. *Iph. Taur.* 1234 foll.    [5] Paus. i. 40.    [6] Paus. i. 34.

chus,[1] Charon,[2] Pasiphae,[3] Herakles,[4] Dionysus,[5] and above all Asklepios,[6] gave answers after this fashion, mainly, but not entirely, in cases of sickness. The prevalence of heroes, rather than gods, as the givers of oracles in dreams seems still further to indicate the immediate derivation of this form of revelation from the accustomed appearance of departed friends in sleep.

The next step takes us to the most celebrated class of oracles,—those in which the prophetess, or more rarely the prophet, gives vent in agitated trance to the words which she is inspired to utter.[7] We encounter here the phenomena of possession, so familiar to us in the Bible, and of which theology still maintains the genuineness, while science would explain them by delirium, hysteria, or epilepsy. It

---

[1] Dio Cass. lxxii. 7.

[2] Eustath. *Schol. ad Dionys. Perieg.* 1153.

[3] Cic. *de Div.* i. 43 ; Plut. *Agis* 9, and cf. Maury, ii. 453.

[4] Paus. ix. 24, comp. inscr. ap. G. Wolff, *de Noviss.* p. 29, and see Plut. *de Malign. Herod.* 31, for the dream of Leonidas in Herakles' temple.                           [5] Paus. x. 33.

[6] Ar. Rhet. *passim ;* Iambl. *Myst.* 3, 3, etc.   See also Val. Max. i. 7 ; Diod. Sic. v. 62 ; Ar. Rhet. *Sacr. Serm.* iii. 311, for dreams sent by Athene, the Soteres, Hemithea.   Further references will be found in Maury, iii. 456, and for the relation of Apollo to dreams see Bouché-Leclercq, i. 204.

[7] Pindar's phrase (for the prophecy of Iamus), φωνὰν ἀκούειν ψευδέων ἄγνωστον, *Ol.* vi. 66, reminds us of Socrates' inward monitor. The expressions used about the Pythia vary from this conception of mere *clairaudience* to the idea of an absolute *possession*, which for the time holds the individuality of the prophetess entirely in abeyance.

was this phenomenon, connected first, as Pausanias tells us,[1] with the Apolline oracles, which gave a wholly new impressiveness to oracular replies. No longer confined to simple affirmation and negation, or to the subjective and ill-remembered utterances of a dream, they were now capable of embracing all topics, and of being preserved in writing as a revelation of general applicability. These oracles of inspiration, — taken in connection with the oracles uttered by visible phantoms, which become prominent at a later era,—may be considered as marking the highest point of development to which Greek oracles attained. It will be convenient to defer our consideration of some of these phenomena till we come to the great controversy between Porphyry and Eusebius, in which they were for the first time fully discussed. But there is one early oracle of the dead, different in some respects from any that succeeded it,[2] which presents so many points for notice that a

---

[1] Paus. i. 34. We should have expected this prophetic frenzy to have been connected with Bacchus or the Nymphs rather than with Apollo, and it is possible that there may have been some transference of the phenomena from the one worship to the other. The causes which have determined the attributes of the Greek deities are often too fanciful to admit of explanation now.

[2] The distinction drawn by Nägelsbach between this and other "Todtenorakeln" (*Nachhom. Theologie*, p. 189) is surely exaggerated. See Klausen, *Aeneas und die Penaten*, p. 129 foll., for other legends connecting Odysseus with early necromancy, and on this general subject see Herod. v. 92; Eur. *Alc.* 1131; Plat. *Leg.* x. 909; Plut. *Cim.* 6, *de Ser. Num. Vind.* 17; Tylor, *Prim. Cult.* ii. 41. The fact, on which Nägelsbach dwells, that Odysseus, after

few reflections on the state of belief which it indicates will assist us in comprehending the nature of the elevation of Greek faith which was afterwards effected under the influence of Delphi.

For this,—the first oracle of which we have a full account, — the descent of Odysseus to the underworld, "to consult the soul of the Theban Teiresias," shows in a way which it would be hard to parallel elsewhere the possible co-existence in the same mind of the creed and practices of the lowest races with a majesty, a pathos, a power, which human genius has never yet overpassed. The eleventh book of the Odyssey is steeped in the Animism of barbarous peoples. The Cimmerian entrance to the world of souls is the close parallel (to take one instance among many) of the extreme western cape of Vanua Levi, a calm and solemn place of cliff and forest, where the souls of the Fijian dead embark for the judgment-seat of Ndengei, and whither the living come on pilgrimage, thinking to see ghosts and gods.[1]   Homer's ghosts cheep and twitter precisely as the shadow-

consulting Teiresias, satisfied his affection and his curiosity by interviews with other ghosts in no way alters the original injunction laid on him, the purport of his journey—ψυχῇ χρησόμενον Θηβαίου Τειρεσίαο. Nägelsbach's other argument, that in later times we hear only of a dream-oracle, not an apparition-oracle, of Teiresias seems to me equally weak. Readers of Pausanias must surely feel what a chance it is which has determined the oracles of which we *have* heard.

    [1] *Prim. Cult.* i. 408.

souls of the Algonquin Indians chirp like crickets, and Polynesian spirits speak in squeaking tones, and the accent of the ancestral Zulu, when he reappears on earth, has earned for him the name of Whistler.[1] The expedition of Odysseus is itself paralleled by the exploit of Ojibwa, the eponymous hero of the Ojibbeways, of the Finnish hero Wainamoinen, and of many another savage chief.  The revival of the ghosts with blood, itself closely paralleled in old Teutonic mythologies,[2] speaks of the time when the soul is conceived as feeding on the fumes and sha- dows of earthly food, as when the Chinese beat the drum which summons ancestral souls to supper, and provide a pail of gruel and a spoon for the greater convenience of any ancestor who may unfortunately have been deprived of his head.[3]

Nay, even the inhabitants of that underworld are only the semblances of once living men. " They them- selves," in the terrible words of the opening sentence of the Iliad, " have been left a prey to dogs and every bird."  Human thought has not yet reached a point at which spirit could be conceived of as more than the shadow of matter.

And if further evidence were needed, the oracle of Teiresias himself—opening like a chasm into Hades through the sunlit soil of Greece—reveals unwittingly all the sadness which underlies that freshness and power, the misgiving which so often

[1] *Prim. Cult.* ii. 42.    [2] *Ibid.* ii. 346.    [3] *Ibid.* ii. 30.

unites the savage and the philosopher, the man who comes before religions and the man who comes after them, in the gloom of the same despair. Himself alone in his wisdom among the ineffectual shades, Teiresias offers to Odysseus, in the face of all his unjust afflictions, no prevention and no cure; "of honey-sweet return thou askest, but by God's will bitter shall it be;"—for life's struggle he has no remedy but to struggle to the end, and for the wandering hero he has no deeper promise than the serenity of a gentle death.

And yet Homer "made the theogony of the Greeks."[1]  And Homer, through the great ages which followed him, not only retained, but deepened his hold on the Hellenic spirit. It was no mere tradition, it was the ascendency of that essential truth and greatness in Homer, which we still so strongly feel, which was the reason why he was clung to and invoked and explained and allegorised by the loftiest minds of Greece in each successive age; why he was transformed by Polygnotus, transformed by Plato, transformed by Porphyry. Nay, even in our own day,—and this is not the least significant fact in religious history,—we have seen one of the most dominant, one of the most religious intellects of our century, falling under the same spell, and extracting from Homer's almost savage

---

[1] Herod. ii. 53, οὗτοι δέ (Homer and Hesiod) εἰσι οἱ ποιήσαντες θεογονίην Ἕλλησι, κ.τ. λ.

animism the full-grown mysteries of the Christian faith.

So dangerous would it be to assume such a congruence throughout the whole mass of the thought of any epoch, however barbarous, that the baseness or falsity of some of its tenets should be enough to condemn the rest unheard. So ancient, so innate in man is the power of apprehending by emotion and imagination aspects of reality for which a deliberate culture might often look in vain. To the dictum,—so true though apparently so paradoxical,—which asserts "that the mental condition of the lower races is the key to poetry," we may reply with another apparent paradox—that poetry is the only thing which every age is certain to recognise as truth.

Having thus briefly considered the nature of each of the main classes of oracular response, it is natural to go on to some inquiry into the history of the leading shrines where these responses were given. The scope of this essay does not admit of a detailed notice of each of the very numerous oracular seats of which some record has reached us.[1] But before passing on to Delphi, I must dwell on two cases of special interest, where recent explorations have brought us nearer than elsewhere to what may be

[1] The number of Greek oracular seats, with the Barbarian seats known to the Greeks, has been estimated at 260, or an even larger number; but of very many of these we know no more than the name.

called the private business of an oracle, or to the actual structure of an Apolline sanctuary.

The oracle of Zeus at Dodona takes the highest place among all the oracles which answered by signs rather than by inspired speech.[1]  It claimed to be the eldest of all, and we need not therefore wonder that its phenomena present an unusual confluence of streams of primitive belief.  The first mention of Dodona,[2]—in that great invocation of Achilles which is one of the glimpses which Homer gives us of a world far earlier than his own,—seems to indicate that it was then a seat of dream-oracles, where the rude Selloi perhaps drew from the earth on which they slept such visions as she sends among men. But in the Odyssey[3] and in Hesiod[4] the oracle is spoken of as having its seat among the leaves, or in the hollow or base of an oak, and this is the idea which prevailed in classical times.[5]  The doves,[6]— if doves there were, and not merely priestesses, whose name, Peleiades, may be derived from some other root,[7]—introduce another element of complexity.

<hr/>

[1] Strab. viii. *Fragm.* ἐχρησμῴδει δ' οὐ διὰ λόγων ἀλλὰ διά τινων συμβόλων, ὥσπερ τὸ ἐν Λιβύῃ Ἀμμωνιακόν.  So Suid. *in voc.* Δωδώνη, etc.        [2] *Il.* xvi. 233.

[3] *Od.* xiv. 327, xix. 296.

[4] Hes. *Fr.* 39. 7, ναῖον τ' ἐν πυθμένι φηγοῦ.  See Plat. *Phaedr.* 275.

[5] Aesch. *Prom.* 832 ; Soph. *Trach.* 172 and 1167.

[6] See Herod. ii. 54, and comp. *Od.* xii. 63.

[7] See Herm. *Griech. Antiq.* ii. 250.  Dr. Robertson Smith suggests " that the Dove-soothsayers were so named from their *croon* . . . and that the μέλισσα (the Pythia) in like manner is the humming priestess." —*Journal of Philology*, vol. xiv. p. 120.

Oracles were also given at Dodona by means of
lots,[1] and by the falling of water.[2] Moreover, German industry has established the fact, that at
Dodona it thunders on more days than anywhere
else in Europe, and that no peals are louder anywhere
than those which echo among the Acroceraunian
mountains.　It is tempting to derive the word
Dodona from the sound of a thunderclap, and to
associate this old Pelasgic sanctuary with the pro-
pitiation of elemental deities in their angered hour.[3]
But the notices of the oracle in later days are per-
plexingly at variance with all these views.　They
speak mainly of oracles given by the sound of caldrons, — struck, according to Strabo,[4] by knuckle-

---

[1] Cic. *de Div.* ii. 32.　　　　[2] Serv. *ad Aen.* iii. 466.

[3] I do not think that we can get beyond some such vague conjecture as this, and A. Mommsen and Schmidt's elaborate calculations as to months of maximum frequency of thunderclaps and
centres of maximum frequency of earthquakes, as determining the
time of festivals or the situation of oracular temples, seem to me
to be quite out of place. If a savage possessed the methodical
patience of a German observer, he would be a savage no more.
*Savants* must be content to leave Aristotle's τύχη καὶ τὸ αὐτόματον,
—chance and spontaneity,—as causes of a large part of the action
of primitive men.

The dictum of Götte (*Delphische Orakel,* p. 13) seems to me
equally unproveable : "Dodona, wohin die schwarzen aegyptischen
Tauben geflogen kamen, ist wohl unbestreitbar eine aegyptische
Cultstätte, die Schwesteranstalt von Ammonium, beide Thebens
Töchter." The geographical position of Dodona is much against
this view, the doves are very problematical, and the possible ex-
istence of a primitive priesthood in the Selloi is no proof of an
Egyptian influence.

[4] Strab. lib. vii. *Fragm.* ap. Hermann, *Griech. Ant.* ii. 251,
where see further citations.

bones attached to a wand held by a statue. The temple is even said to have been *made* of caldrons,[1] or at least they were so arranged, as a certain Demon tells us,[2] that "all in turn, when one was smitten, the caldrons of Dodona rang." The perpetual sound thus caused is alluded to in a triumphant tone by other writers,[3] but it is the more difficult to determine in what precise way the will of Zeus was understood.

Among such a mass of traditions, it is of course easy to find analogies. The doves may be compared to the hissing ducks of the Abipones, which were connected with the souls of the dead,[4] or with the

[1] Steph. Byz. *s. voc.* Δωδώνη, quoted by Carapanos, in whose monograph on Dodona citations on all these points will be found.

[2] Müller, *Fragm. Hist. Gr.* iii. 125.

[3] Callim. *Hymn. in Del.* 286 ; Philostr. *Imag.* ii. 33 (a slightly different account).

[4] *Prim. Cult.* ii. 6. The traces of animal worship in Greece are many and interesting, but are not closely enough connected with our present subject to be discussed at length. Apollo's possible characters, as the Wolf, the Locust, or the Fieldmouse (or the Slayer of wolves, of locusts, or of fieldmice), have not perceptibly affected his oracles. Still less need we be detained by the fish-tailed Eurynome, or the horse-faced Demeter (Paus. viii. 41, 42). And although from the time when the boy-prophet Iamus lay among the wall-flowers, and "the two bright-eyed serpents fed him with the harmless poison of the bee" (Pind. *Ol.* vi. 28), snakes appear frequently in connection with prophetic power, their worship falls under the head of divination rather than of oracles. The same remark may be made of ants, cats, and cows. The bull Apis occupies a more definite position, but though he was visited by Greeks, his worship was not a product of Greek thought. The nearest Greek approach, perhaps, to an animal-oracle was at the fount of Myræ in Cilicia (Plin. *H.N.* xxxii. 2), where fish swam up to eat or reject the food thrown to them. "Diripere eos carnes objectas

doves in Popayan, which are spared as inspired by departed souls. The tree-worship opens up lines of thought too well known for repetition. We may liken the Dodonæan "voiceful oak" to the tamarisks of Beersheba, and the oak of Shechem,—its whisper to the "sound of a going in the tops of the mulberry-trees," which prompted Israel to war,[1] and so on down the long train of memories to Joan of Arc hanging with garlands the fairies' beech in the woods of Domremy, and telling her persecutors that if they would set her in a forest once more she would hear the heavenly voices plain.[2] Or we may prefer, with another school, to trace this tree also back to the legendary Ygdrassil, "the celestial tree of the Aryan family," with its spreading branches of the stratified clouds of heaven. One legend at least points to the former interpretation as the more natural. For just as a part of the ship Argo, keel or prow, was made of the Dodonæan oak, and Argo's crew heard with astonishment the ship herself prophesy to them on the sea :—

laetum est consultantibus," says Pliny, "caudis abigere dirum." The complaint of a friend of Plutarch's (*Quæst. conviv.* iv. 4) "that it was impossible to obtain from fishes a single instructive look or sound," is thus seen to have been exaggerated. And it appears that live snakes were kept in the cave of Trophonius (Philostr. *Vit. Apoll.* viii. 19), in order to inspire terror in visitors, who were instructed to appease them with cakes (Suid. *s. v. μελιτοῦττα*).

[1] 2 Sam. v. 24.

[2] "Dixit quod si esset in uno nemore bene audiret voces venientes ad eam."—On Tree-worship, see Lubbock, *Origin of Civilisation,* p. 206 foll.

"But Jason and the builder, Argus, knew
   Whereby the prow foretold things strange and new ;
   Nor wondered aught, but thanked the gods therefore,
   As far astern they left the Mysian shore," [1]—

so do we find a close parallel to this among the Siamese,[2] who believe that the inhabiting nymphs of trees pass into the guardian spirits of boats built with their wood, to which they continue to sacrifice.

Passing on to the answers which were given at this shrine, we find that at Dodona,[3] as well as at Delphi,[4] human sacrifice is to be discerned in the background. But in the form in which the legend reaches us, its horror has been sublimed into pathos. Coresus, priest of Bacchus at Calydon, loved the maiden Callirhoe in vain. Bacchus, indignant at his servant's repulse, sent madness and death on Calydon. The oracle of Dodona announced that Coresus must sacrifice Callirhoe, or some one who would die for her. No one was willing to die for her, and she stood up beside the altar to be slain. But when Coresus looked on her his love overcame his anger, and he slew himself in her stead. Then her heart turned to him, and beside the fountain to which her name was given she died by her own hand, and followed him to the underworld.

---

[1] Morris' *Life and Death of Jason*, Book iv. *ad fin.*
[2] *Prim. Cult.* ii. 198.     [3] Paus. vii. 21.
[4] Eus. *Pr. Ev.* v. 27, παρθένον Αἰπυτίδαν κλῆρος καλεῖ, etc. See also the romantic story of Melanippus and Comætho, Paus. vii. 19.

There is another legend of Dodona[1] to which
the student of oracles may turn with a certain grim
satisfaction at the thought that the ambiguity of
style which has so often baffled him did once at
least carry its own penalty with it. Certain Bœotian
envoys, so the story runs, were told by Myrtile, the
priestess of Dodona, "that it would be best for them
to do the most impious thing possible." The Bœotians immediately threw the priestess into a caldron
of boiling water, remarking that they could not think
of anything much more impious than *that*.

The ordinary business of Dodona, however, was
of a less exciting character. M. Carapanos has discovered many tablets on which the inquiries of
visitors to the oracle were inscribed, and these give
a picture, sometimes grotesque, but oftener pathetic,
of the simple faith of the rude Epirots who dwelt
round about the shrine. The statuette of an acrobat
hanging to a rope shows that the "Dodonæan Pelas-
gian Zeus" did not disdain to lend his protection to
the least dignified forms of jeopardy to life and limb.
A certain Agis asks "whether he has lost his
blankets and pillows himself, or some one outside
has stolen them." An unknown woman asks simply
how she may be healed of her disease. Lysanias
asks if he is indeed the father of the child which
his wife Nyla is soon to bear. Evandrus and his

[1] Ephor. ad Strab. ix. 2 ; Heracl. Pont. *Fragm. Hist. Gr.* ii. 198 ;
Proclus, *Chrest.* ii. 248, and see Carapanos.

wife, in broken dialect, seek to know "by what prayer or worship they may fare best now and for ever." And there is something strangely pathetic in finding on a broken plate of lead the imploring inquiry of the fierce and factious Corcyreans,—made, alas! in vain,—"to what god or hero offering prayer and sacrifice they might live together in unity?"[1] "For the men of that time," says Plato,[2] "since they were not wise as ye are nowadays, it was enough in their simplicity to listen to oak or rock, if only these told them true." To those rude tribes, indeed, their voiceful trees were the one influence which lifted them above barbarism and into contact with the surrounding world. Again and again Dodona was ravaged,[3] but so long as the oak was standing the temple rose anew. When at last an Illyrian bandit cut down the oak[4] the presence of Zeus was gone, and the desolate Thesprotian valley has known since then no other sanctity, and has found no other voice.

I proceed to another oracular seat, of great mythical celebrity, though seldom alluded to in classical times, to which a recent exploration[5] has given a striking interest, bringing us, as it were, into direct connection across so many ages with the birth and advent of a god.

[1] Τίνι κα θεῶν ἢ ἡρώων θύοντες καὶ ὠχόμενοι ὁμονοοῖεν ἐπὶ τἀγαθόν.
[2] Phaedr. 275.
[3] Strab. vii. 6; Polyb. ix. 67, and cf. Wolff, *de Noviss.* p. 13.
[4] Serv. *ad Aen.* iii. 466.
[5] *Recherches sur Délos*, par J. A. Lebègue, 1876.

On the slope of Cynthus, near the mid-point of
the Isle of Delos, ten gigantic blocks of granite,
covered with loose stones and the débris of ages,
form a rude vault, half hidden in the hill.   The
islanders call it the "dragon's cave;" travellers had
taken it for the remains of a fortress or of a reser-
voir.   It was reserved for two French savants to
show how much knowledge the most familiar texts
have yet to yield when they are meditated on by
minds prepared to compare and to comprehend.   A
familiar passage in Homer,[1] illustrated by much
ancient learning and by many calculations of his
own, suggested to M. Burnouf, Director of the French
School of Archæology at Athens, that near this point
had been a primitive post of observation of the
heavens; nay, that prehistoric men had perhaps
measured their seasons by the aid of some rude
instrument in this very cave.   An equally familiar
line of Virgil,[2] supported by some expressions in a
Homeric hymn, led M. Lebègue to the converging
conjecture that at this spot the Delian oracle had
its seat; that here it was that Leto's long wanderings ended, and Apollo and Artemis were born.
Every schoolboy has learnt by heart the sounding
lines which tell how Aeneas "venerated the temple
built of ancient stone," and how at the god's unseen
coming "threshold and laurel trembled, and all the

---

[1] *Od.* xv. 403.   Em. Burnouf, *Revue Archéologique*, Aug. 8, 1873.
[2] *Aen.* iii. 84; Hom. *Hymn. Del.* 15-18, and 79-81.

mountain round about was moved." But M. Lebègue
was the first to argue hence with confidence that the
oracle must have been upon the mountain and not
on the coast, and that those ancient stones, like the
Cyclopean treasure-house of Mycenæ, might be found
and venerated still. So far as a reader can judge
without personal survey, these expectations have
been amply fulfilled.[1] At each step M. Lebègue's
researches revealed some characteristic of an oracular
shrine. In a walled external space were the remains of a marble base on which a three-legged
instrument had been fixed by metal claws. Then
came a transverse wall, shutting off the temple
within, which looks westward, so that the worshipper,
as he approaches, may face the east. The floor of
this temple is reft by a chasm,—the continuation of
a ravine which runs down the hill, and across which
the sanctuary has been intentionally built. And in
the inner recess is a rough block of granite, smoothed
on the top, where a statue has stood. The statue
has probably been knocked into the chasm by a rock
falling through the partly-open roof. Its few fragments show that it represented a young god. The
stone itself is probably a fetish, surviving, with the
Cyclopean stones which make the vault above it,

[1] M. Homolle (*Fouilles de Délos*, 1879) gives no direct opinion
on the matter, but his researches indirectly confirm M. Lebègue's
view, in so far as that among the numerous inscriptions, etc., which
he has found among the ruins of the temple of Apollo on the coast,
there seems to be no trace of oracular response or inquiry.

from a date perhaps many centuries before the
Apolline religion came. This is all, but this is
enough. For we have here in narrow compass all
the elements of an oracular shrine; the westward
aspect, the sacred enclosure, the tripod, the sanctuary, the chasm, the fetish-stone, the statue of a
youthful god. And when the situation is taken into
account, the correspondence with the words both of
Virgil and of the Homerid becomes so close as to be
practically convincing. It is true that the smallness
of scale,—the sanctuary measures some twenty feet
by ten,—and the remote archaism of the structure,
from which all that was beautiful, almost all that
was Hellenic, has long since disappeared, cause at
first a shock of disappointment like that inspired by
the size of the citadel, and the character of the
remains at Hissarlik. Yet, on reflection, this seem-
ing incongruity is an additional element of proof.
There is something impressive in the thought that
amidst all the marble splendour which made Delos
like a jewel in the sea, it was this cavernous and
prehistoric sanctuary, as mysterious to Greek eyes
as to our own, which their imagination identified
with that earliest temple which Leto promised, in
her hour of trial, that Apollo's hands should build.
This, the one remaining seat of oracle out of the
hundreds which Greece contained, was the one sanctuary which the Far-darter himself had wrought;—
no wonder that his mighty workmanship has out-

lasted the designs of men! All else is gone. The
temples, the amphitheatres, the colonnades, which
glittered on every crest and coign of the holy island,
have sunk into decay. But he who sails among the
isles of Greece may still watch around sea-girt Delos
"the dark wave welling shoreward beneath the shrill
and breezy air;"[1] he may still note at sunrise, as on
that sunrise when the god was born, "the whole
island abloom with shafts of gold, as a hill's crested
summit blooms with woodland flowers."[2] "And
thou thyself, lord of the silver bow," he may exclaim
with the Homerid in that burst of exultation in
which the uniting Ionian race seems to leap to the
consciousness of all its glory in an hour,—"thou
walkedst here in very presence, on Cynthus' leafy
crown!"

> "Ah, many a forest, many a peak is thine,
>     On many a promontory stands thy shrine,
>     But best and first thy love, thy home, is here;
>     Of all thine isles thy Delian isle most dear;—
>     There the long-robed Ionians, man and maid,
>     Press to thy feast in all their pomp arrayed,—
>     To thee, to Artemis, to Leto pay
>     The heartfelt honour on thy natal day;—
>     Immortal would he deem them, ever young,
>     Who then should walk the Ionian folk among,
>     Should those tall men, those stately wives behold,
>     Swift ships seafaring and long-garnered gold:—

---

[1] *Hymn. Del.* 27.                    [2] *Ibid.* 138-164.

But chiefliest far his eyes and ears would meet
Of sights, of sounds most marvellously sweet,
The Delian girls amid the thronging stir,
The loved hand-maidens of the Far-darter;
The Delian girls, whose chorus, long and long,
Chants to the god his strange, his ancient song,—
Till whoso hears it deems his own voice sent
Thro' the azure air that music softly blent,
So close it comes to each man's heart, and so
His own soul feels it and his glad tears flow."

Such was the legend of the indigenous, the Hellenic Apollo. But the sun does not rise over one horizon alone, and the glory of Delos was not left uncontested or unshared. Another hymn, of inferior poetical beauty, but of equal, if not greater, authority among the Greeks, relates how Apollo descended from the Thessalian Olympus, and sought a place where he might found his temple: how he was refused by Tilphussa, and selected Delphi; and how, in the guise of a dolphin, he led thither a crew of Cretans to be the servants of his shrine. With this hymn, so full of meaning for the comparative mythologist, we are here only concerned as introducing us to Apollo in the aspect in which we know him best, "giving his answers from the laurel-wood, beneath the hollows of Parnassus' hill."[1]

At Delphi, as at Dodona, we seem to trace the relics of many a form of worship and divination which we cannot now distinctly recall. From that

---

[1] *Hymn. Pyth.* 214.

deep cleft "in rocky Pytho," Earth, the first prophetess, gave her earliest oracle,[1] in days which were
already a forgotten antiquity to the heroic age of
Greece. The maddening vapour, which was supposed
to rise from the chasm,[2] belongs to nymph-inspira-
tion rather than to the inspiration of Apollo. At
Delphi, too, was the most famous of all fetish-
stones, believed in later times to be the centre of
the earth.[3]  At Delphi divination from the sacrifice
of goats reached an immemorial antiquity.[4]  Delphi,
too, was an ancient centre of divination by fire, a
tradition which survived in the name of Pyrcon,[5]
given to Hephaestus' minister, while Hephaestus
shared with Earth the possession of the shrine, and
in the mystic title of the Flame-kindlers,[6] assigned
in oracular utterances to the Delphian folk. At
Delphi, too, in ancient days, the self-moved lots

[1] Aesch. *Eum.* 2 ; Paus. x. 5 ; cf. Eur. *Iph. Taur.* 1225 *sqq.*

[2] Strabo, ix. p. 419, etc. In a paper read before the British
Archæological Association, March 5, 1879, Dr. Phenè has given an
interesting account of subterranean chambers at Delphi, which
seem to indicate that gases from the subterranean Castalia were
received in a chamber where the Pythia may have sat. But in the
absence of direct experiment this whole question is physiologically
very obscure. It is even possible, as M. Bouché-Leclercq urges,
that the Pythia's frenzy may be a survival from a previous
Dionysiac worship at Delphi, and thus originally traceable to a
quite orthodox intoxicant.

[3] Paus. x. 16, etc.

[4] Diod. Sic. xvi. 26. Pliny (*Hist. Nat.* vii. 56) ascribes the in
vention of this mode of divination to Delphos, a son of Apollo.

[5] Paus. x. 5.

[6] Plut. *Pyth.* 24.

sprang in the goblet in obedience to Apollo's will.[1]
The waving of the Delphic laurel,[2] which in later
times seemed no more than a token of the wind and
spiritual stirring which announced the advent of
the god, was probably the relic of an ancient tree-
worship, like that of Dodona,[3] and Daphne, priestess
of Delphi's primeval Earth-oracle,[4] is but one more
of the old symbolical figures that have melted back
again into impersonal nature at the appearing of
the God of Day.　Lastly, at Delphi is laid the
scene of the sharpest conflict between the old gods
and the new.　Whatever may have been the meaning of the Python,—whether he were a survival of
snake-worship, or a winding stream which the sun's
rays dry into rotting marsh, or only an emblem of
the cloud which trails across the sunlit heaven,—
his slaughter by Apollo was an integral part of the
early legend, and at the Delphian festivals the
changes of the " Pythian strain " commemorated for
many a year that perilous encounter,—the god's
descent into the battlefield, his shout of summons,

---

[1] Suidas, iii. p. 237; cf. Callim. *Hymn. in Apoll.* 45, etc.

[2] Ar. *Plut.* 213 ; Callim. *Hymn. in Apoll.* 1, etc.

[3] I cannot, however, follow M. Maury (*Religions de la Grèce*, ii.
442) in supposing (as he does in the case of the Delian laurel, *Aen.*
iii. 73) that such tree-movements need indicate an ancient habit of
divining from their sound.　The idea of a wind accompanying
divine manifestations seems more widely diffused in Greece than
the Dodonæan idea of vocal trees. Cf. (for instance) Plut. *De Def.*
*orac.* of the Delphian adytum, εὐωδίας ἀναπίμπλαται καὶ πνεύματος.

[4] Paus. x. 5.

his cry of conflict, his paean of victory, and then
the gnashing of the dragon's teeth in his fury, the
hiss of his despair.[1]  And the mythology of a later
age has connected with this struggle the first ideas
of moral conflict and expiation which the new
religion had to teach; has told us that the victor
needed purification after his victory; that he endured and was forgiven; and that the god himself
first wore his laurel-wreath as a token of supplica-
tion, and not of song.[2]

With a similar ethical purpose the simple narrative of the Homerid has been transformed into a
legend[3] of a type which meets us often in the
middle ages, but which wears a deeper pathos when
it occurs in the midst of Hellenic gladness and
youth,—the legend of Trophonius and Agamedes,
the artificers who built the god's home after his
heart's desire, and whom he rewarded with the
guerdon that is above all other recompense, a speedy
and a gentle death.

In the new temple at any rate, as rebuilt in
historic times, the moral significance of the Apolline
religion was expressed in unmistakable imagery.
Even as "four great zones of sculpture" girded the
hall of Camelot, the centre of the faith which was

---

[1] ἄμπειρα, κατακελευσμός, σάλπιγξ, δάκτυλοι, ὀδοντισμός, σύριγγες.
See August Mommsen's *Delphika* on this topic.

[2] Bötticher, *Baumcultus*, p. 353; and see reff. ap. Herm. *Griech.
Ant.* ii. 127. Cf. Eur. *Ion*, 114 *sqq.*

[3] Cic. *Tusc.* i. 47; cf. Plut. *De Consol. ad Apollon.* 14.

civilising Britain, "with many a mystic symbol" of
the victory of man; so over the portico of the Delphian god were painted or sculptured such scenes as
told of the triumph of an ideal humanity over the
monstrous deities which are the offspring of savage
fear.[1]

There was "the light from the eyes of the twin
faces" of Leto's children; there was Herakles with
golden sickle, Iolaus with burning brand, withering
the heads of the dying Hydra,—"the story," says
the girl in the *Ion* who looks thereon, "which is
sung beside my loom;" there was the rider of the
winged steed slaying the fire-breathing Chimaera;
there was the tumult of the giants' war; Pallas
lifting the aegis against Enceladus; Zeus crushing
Mimas with the great bolt fringed with flame, and
Bacchus "with his unwarlike ivy-wand laying
another of Earth's children low."

It is important thus to dwell on some of the
indications,—and there are many of them,—which
point to the conviction entertained in Greece as to
the ethical and civilising influence of Delphi, inasmuch as the responses which have actually been
preserved to us, though sufficient, when attentively
considered, to support this view, are hardly such as
would at once have suggested it.  The set collections

[1] The passage in the *Ion*, 190-218, no doubt describes either the
portico which the Athenians dedicated at Delphi about 426 B.C.
(Paus. x. 11), or (as the words of the play, if taken strictly, would
indicate) the façade of the temple itself.

of oracles, which no doubt contained those of most ethical importance, have perished; of all the "dark-written tablets, groaning with many an utterance of Loxias,"[1] none remain to us except such fragments of Porphyry's treatise as Eusebius has embodied in his refutation.   And many of the oracles which we do possess owe their preservation to the most trivial causes,—to their connection with some striking anecdote, or to something quaint in their phraseology which has helped to make them proverbial.   The reader, therefore, who passes from the majestic descriptions of the *Ion* or the *Eumenides* to the actual study of the existing oracles will at first run much risk of disappointment.   Both style and subject will often seem unworthy of these lofty claims. He will come, for instance, on such oracles as that which orders Temenus to seek as guide of the army a man with three eyes, who turns out (according to different legends) to be either a one-eyed man on a two-eyed horse, or a two-eyed man on a one-eyed mule.[2]   This oracle is composed precisely on the model of the primitive riddles of the Aztec and the Zulu, and is almost repeated in Scandinavian legend, where Odin's single eye gives point to the enigma.[3] Again, the student's ear will often be offended by

---

[1] Eur. *Fr.* 625.   Collections of oracles continued to be referred to till the Turks took Constantinople, *i.e.* for about 2000 years. See reff. ap. Wolff, *de Noviss.* p. 48.

[2] Apollod. ii. 8; Paus. v. 3.          [3] *Prim. Cult.* i. 85.

roughnesses of rhythm which seem unworthy of the divine inventor of the hexameter.[1]　And the constantly-recurring prophecies are, for the most part, uninteresting and valueless, as the date of their composition cannot be proved, nor their genuineness in any way tested.　As an illustration of the kind of difficulties which we here encounter, we may select one remarkable oracle,[2] of immense celebrity in antiquity, which certainly suggests more questions than we can readily answer.　The outline of the familiar story is as follows :—Crœsus wished to make war on Cyrus, but was afraid to do so without express sanction from heaven.　It was therefore all-important to him to test the veracity of the oracles, and his character, as the most religious man of his time, enabled him to do so systematically, without risk of incurring the charge of impiety. He sent messages to the six best-known oracles then existing,—to Delphi, to Dodona, to Branchidae, to the oracles of Zeus Ammon, of Trophonius, of Amphiaraus.　On the hundredth day from leaving Sardis, his envoys were to ask what Crœsus was at that moment doing.　Four oracles failed ; Amphi-

---

[1] Bald though the god's style may often be, he possesses at any rate a sounder notion of metre than some of his German critics. Lobeck (*Aglaophamus*, p. 852), attempting to restore a lost response, suggests the line

στεννγρὴν δ'ἐνοεῦν εὐρυγάστορα οὐ κατὰ γαῖαν.

He apologises for the quantity of the first syllable of εὐρυγάστορα, but seems to think that no further remark is needed.

[2] Herod. i. 47.

araus was nearly right; Apollo at Delphi entirely succeeded. For the Pythia answered, with exact truth, that Crœsus was engaged in boiling a lamb and a tortoise together in a copper vessel with a copper lid. The messengers, who had not themselves known what Crœsus was going to do, returned to Sardis and reported, and were then once more despatched to Delphi, with gifts so splendid that in the days of Herodotus they were still the glory of the sanctuary. They now asked the practically important question as to going to war, and received a quibbling answer which, in effect, lured on Crœsus to his destruction.

Now here the two things certain are that Crœsus did send these gifts to Delphi, and did go to war with Cyrus. Beyond these facts there is no sure footing. Short and pithy fragments of poetry, like the oracles on which the story hangs, are generally among the earliest and most enduring fragments of genuine history. On the other hand, they are just the utterances which later story-tellers are most eager to invent. Nor must we argue from their characteristic diction, for the pseudo-oracular is a style which has in all ages been cultivated with success. The fact which it is hardest to dispose of is the existence of the prodigious, the unrivalled offerings of Crœsus at Delphi. Why were they sent there, unless for some such reason as Herodotus gives? Or are they sufficiently ex-

plained by a mere reference to that almost superstitious deference with which the Mermnadae seem
to have regarded the whole religion and civilisation
of Greece?  With our imperfect data, we can perhaps hardly go with safety beyond the remark that,
granting the genuineness of the oracle about the
tortoise, and the substantial truth of Herodotus'
account, there will still be no reason to suppose
that the god had any foreknowledge as to the result
of Crœsus' war.  The story itself, in fact, contains
almost a proof to the contrary.  We cannot suppose
that the god, in saying, " Crœsus, if he cross the
Halys, shall undo a mighty realm," was intentionally inciting his favoured servant to his ruin.  It is
obvious that he was sheltering his ignorance behind
a calculated ambiguity.  And the only intelligence
to which he or his priestess could, on any hypothesis,
fairly lay claim, would be of the kind commonly
described as " second-sight," a problem with which
ethnologists have already to deal all over the world,
from the Hebrides to the Coppermine River.

It is obvious that the documents before us are
far from enabling us to prove even this hypothesis
And we are farther still from any evidence for
actual prophecy which can stand a critical investi-
gation.  Hundreds of such cases are indeed reported
to us, and it was on a conviction that Apollo did
indeed foretell the future that the authority of
Delphi mainly depended.  But when we have said

this, we have said all; no case is so reported as to
enable us altogether to exclude the possibility of
coincidence, or of the fabrication of the prophecy
after the event.    But, on the other hand,—and this
is a more surprising circumstance,—it is equally
difficult to get together any satisfactory evidence for
the conjecture which the parallel between Delphi
and the Papacy so readily suggests, — that the
power of the oracle was due to the machinations of
a priestly aristocracy, with widely-scattered agents,
who insinuated themselves into the confidence, and
traded on the credulity, of mankind.    We cannot
but suppose that, to some extent at least, this must
have been the case; that when "the Pythia philip-
pised" she reflected the fears of a knot of Delphian
proprietors; that the unerring counsel given to
private persons, on which Plutarch insists, must
have rested, in part at least, on a secret acquaint-
ance with their affairs, possibly acquired in some
cases under the seal of confession.    In the paucity,
however, of  direct evidence to  this effect, our
estimate of the amount of pressure exercised by a
deliberate human agency in determining the policy
of Delphi must rest mainly on our antecedent view
of what is likely to have  been the case, where the
interests involved were of such wide importance.[1]

[1] For this view of the subject, see Hüllmann, *Würdigung des
Delphischen Orakels;* Götte, *Das Delphische Orakel*. August
Mommsen (*Delphika*) takes a somewhat similar view, and calls the
Pythia a "blosse Figurantin," but his erudition has added little

For indeed the political influence of the Delphian oracle, however inspired or guided,—the value to Hellas of this one unquestioned centre of national counsel and national unity, — has always formed one of the most impressive topics with which the historian of Greece has had to deal.   And I shall pass this part of my subject rapidly by, as already familiar to most readers, and shall not repeat at length the well-known stories,—the god's persistent command to expel the Peisistratids from Athens, his partiality for Sparta, as shown both in encouragement and warning,[1] or the attempts, successful[2] and unsuccessful,[3] to bribe his priestess.   Nor shall I do more than allude to the encouragement of colonisation, counsel of great wisdom, which the god lost no opportunity of enforcing on both the Dorian and the Ionian stocks.   He sent the Cretans to Sicily,[4] and Alcmaeon to the Echinades;[5] he ordered the foundation of Byzantium[6] " over against the city of the blind;" he sent Archias to Ortygia to

to the scanty store of texts on which Hüllmann, etc., depend.   I may mention here that Hendess has collected most of the existing oracles (except those quoted by Eusebius) in a tract, *Oracula quae supersunt*, etc., which is convenient for reference.

[1] Herod. vi. 52; Thuc. i. 118, 123; ii. 54.   Warnings, ap. Paus. iii. 8; ix. 32; Diod. Sic. xi. 50; xv. 54.   Plut. *Lys.* 22; *Agesil.* 3.

[2] Cleisthenes, Herod. v. 63, 66; Pleistoanax, Thuc. v. 16.

[3] Lysander; Plut. *Lys.* 26; Ephor. *Fr.* 127; Nep. *Lys.* 3.   See also Herod. vi. 66.

[4] Herod. vii. 170.          [5] Thuc. ii. 102.

[6] Strab. vii. 320; Tac. *Ann.* xii. 63; but see Herod. iv. 144.

found Syracuse,[1] the Bœotians to Heraclea at Pratos,[2] and the Spartans to Heraclea in Thessaly. And in the story which Herodotus[3] and Pindar[4] alike have made renowned, he singled out Battus,— anxious merely to learn a cure for his stammer, but type of the man with a destiny higher than he knows,—to found at Cyrene "a charioteering city upon the silvern bosom of the hill." And, as has often been remarked, this function of colonisation had a religious as well as a political import. The colonists, before whose adventurous armaments Apollo, graven on many a gem, still hovers over the sea, carried with them the civilising maxims of the " just-judging " [5] sanctuary as well as the brand kindled on the world's central altar-stone from that pine-fed [6] and eternal fire. Yet more distinctly can we trace the response of the god to each successive stage of ethical progress to which the evolution of Greek thought attains.

The moralising Hesiod is honoured at Delphi in preference to Homer himself. The Seven Wise Men, the next examples of a deliberate effort after ethical rules, are connected closely with the Pythian shrine. Above the portal is inscribed that first condition of all moral progress, " Know Thyself ";

[1] Paus. v. 7.						[2] Justin. xvi. 3.
[3] Herod. iv. 155.						[4] *Pyth.* iv.
[5] *Pyth.* xi. 9.
[6] Plut. *de El apud Delphos.* Cf. Aesch. *Eum.* 40 ; *Choeph.* 1036.

nor does the god refuse to encourage the sages
whose inferior ethical elevation suggests to them
only such maxims as, "Most men are bad," or
" Never go bail." [1]

Solon and Lycurgus, the spiritual ancestors of
the Athenian and the Spartan types of virtue, receive the emphatic approval of Delphi, and the
"Theban eagle," the first great exponent of the developed faith of Greece, already siding with the
spirit against the letter, and refusing to ascribe to
a divinity any immoral act, already preaching the
rewards and punishments of a future state in strains
of impassioned revelation,—this great poet is dear
above all men to Apollo during his life, and is
honoured for centuries after his death by the priest's
nightly summons, " Let Pindar the poet come in to
the supper of the god." [2]   It is from Delphi that
reverence for oaths, respect for the life of slaves, of
women, of suppliants, derive in great measure their
sanction and strength.[3]   I need only allude to the
well-known story of Glaucus, who consulted the
god to know whether he should deny having received the gold in deposit from his friend, and who
was warned in lines which sounded from end to end
of Greece of the nameless Avenger of the broken

[1] I say nothing *de EI apud Delphos*, about the mystic word
which five of the wise men, or perhaps all seven together, put up
in wooden letters at Delphi, for their wisdom has in this instance
wholly transcended our interpretation.

[2] Paus. ix. 23.              [3] Herod. ii. 134 ; vi. 139, etc.

oath,—whose wish was punished like a deed, and whose family was blotted out. The numerous responses of which this is the type brought home to men's minds the notion of right and wrong, of reward and punishment, with a force and impressiveness which was still new to the Grecian world.

More surprising, perhaps, at so early a stage of moral thought, is the catholicity of the Delphian god, his indulgence towards ceremonial differences or ceremonial offences, his reference of casuistical problems to the test of the inward rightness of the heart.[1] It was the Pythian Apollo who replied to the inquiry, "How best are we to worship the gods?" by the philosophic answer, "After the custom of your country,"[2] and who, if those customs varied, would only bid men choose "the best." It was Apollo who rebuked the pompous sacrifice of the rich Magnesian by declaring his preference for the cake and frankincense which the pious Achæan offered in humbleness of heart.[3] It was Apollo who

---

[1] See, for instance, the story of the young man and the brigands, Ael. *Hist. Var.* iii. 4. 3.

[2] Xen. *Mem.* iv. 3. ἥ τε γὰρ Πυθία νόμῳ πόλεως ἀναιρεῖ ποιοῦντας εὐσεβῶς ἂν ποιεῖν. The Pythia often urged the maintenance or renewal of ancestral rites. Paus. viii. 24, etc.

[3] Theopomp. *Fr.* 283 ; cf. Sopater, *Prolegg. in Aristid. Panath.* p. 740, εὔαδέ μοι χθιξὸς λίβανος, κ.τ.λ. (Wolff, *de Noviss.* p. 5; Lob, *Agl.* 1006), and compare the story of Poseidon (Plut. *de Prof. in Virt.* 12), who first reproached Stilpon in a dream for the cheapness of his offerings, but on learning that he could afford nothing

warned the Greeks not to make superstition an
excuse for cruelty; who testified, by his command-
ing interference, his compassion for human infirmi-
ties, for the irresistible heaviness of sleep,[1] for the
thoughtlessness of childhood,[2] for the bewilderment
of the whirling brain.[3]

Yet the impression which the Delphian oracles
make on the modern reader will depend less on
isolated anecdotes like these than on something of
the style and temper which appears especially in
those responses which Herodotus has preserved,—
something of that delightful mingling of *naïveté*
with greatness, which was the world's irrecoverable
bloom.   What scholar has not smiled over the
god's answer[4] to the colonists who had gone to a
barren island in mistake for Libya, and came back
complaining that Libya was unfit to live in?   He
told them that " if they who had never visited the

better, smiled, and promised to send abundant anchovies.   For the
Delphian god's respect for honest poverty, see Plin. *H. N.* vii. 47.

[1] Evenius.   Herod. ix. 93.

[2] Paus. viii. 23.   This is the case of the Arcadian children who
hung the goddess in play.

[3] Paus. vi. 9 ; Plut. *Romul.* 28 (Cleomedes).   For further instances of the inculcation of mercy, see Thuc. ii. 102 ; Athen. xi.
p. 504.

[4] Herod. iv. 157.   There seems some analogy between this
story and the Norse legend of second-sight, which narrates how
"Mgimund shut up three Finns in a hut for three nights that
they might visit Iceland and inform him of the lie of the country
where he was to settle.   Their bodies became rigid, they sent their
souls on the errand, and awakening after three days, they gave a
description of the Vatnsdael."— *Prim. Cult.* i. 396.

sheep-bearing Libya knew it better than he who *had*, he greatly admired their cleverness." Who has not felt the majesty of the lines which usher in the test-oracle of Croesus with the lofty assertion of the omniscience of heaven?[1] lines which deeply impressed the Greek mind, and whose graven record, two thousand years afterwards, was among the last relics which were found among the ruins of Delphi.[2]

It is Herodotus, if any one, who has caught for us the expression on the living face of Hellas. It is Herodotus whose pencil has perpetuated that flying moment of young unconsciousness when evil itself seemed as if it could leave no stain on her expanding soul, when all her faults were reparable, and all her wounds benign; when we can still feel that in her upward progress all these and more might be forgiven and pass harmless away—

"For the time
Was May-time, and as yet no sin was dreamed."

And through all this vivid and golden scene the Pythian Apollo—"the god," as he is termed with a sort of familiar affection—is the never-failing counsellor and friend. His providence is all the divinity which the growing nation needs. His wisdom is

---

[1] Herod. i. 47.

[2] Cyriac of Ancona, in the sixteenth century, found a slab of marble with the couplet οἶδα τ' ἐγώ, etc., inscribed on it. See Foucart, p. 139.

not inscrutable and absolute, but it is near and
kind; it is like the counsel of a young father to
his eager boy. To strip the oracles from Herodotus' history would be to deprive it of its deepest
unity and its most characteristic charm.

And in that culminating struggle with the barbarians, when the young nation rose, as it were, to
knightly manhood through one great ordeal, how
moving — through all its perplexities — was the
attitude of the god! We may wish, indeed, that
he had taken a firmer tone, that he had not trembled
before the oncoming host, nor needed men's utmost
supplications before he would give a word of hope.
But this is a later view; it is the view of Oenomaus
and Eusebius, rather than of Aeschylus or Herodotus.[1] To the contemporary Greeks it seemed no
shame nor wonder that the national protector,
benignant but not omnipotent, should tremble with
the fortunes of the nation, that all his strength
should scarcely suffice for a conflict in which every
fibre of the forces of Hellas was strained, "as
though men fought upon the earth and gods in
upper air."

And seldom indeed has history shown a scene
so strangely dramatic, never has poetry entered so
deeply into human fates, as in that council at
Athens[2] when the question of absolute surrender

[1] Herod. vii. 139, seems hardly meant to blame the god, though
it praises the Athenians for hoping against hope.
[2] Herod. vii. 143.

or desperate resistance turned on the interpretation which was to be given to the dark utterance of the god. It was an epithet which saved civilisation; it was the one word which blessed the famous islet instead of cursing it altogether, which gave courage for that most fateful battle which the world has known—

> "Thou, holy Salamis, sons of men shalt slay,
>   Or on earth's scattering or ingathering day."

After the great crisis of the Persian war Apollo is at rest.[1] In the tragedians we find him risen high above the attitude of a struggling tribal god. Worshippers surround him, as in the *Ion*, in the spirit of glad self-dedication and holy service; his priestess speaks as in the opening of the *Eumenides*, where the settled majesty of godhead breathes through the awful calm. And now, more magnificent though more transitory than the poet's song, a famous symbolical picture embodies for the remaining generations of Greeks the culminant conception of the religion of Apollo's shrine.

"Not all the treasures," as Homer has it, "which the stone threshold of the Far-darter holds safe within" would now be so precious to us as the power of looking for one hour on the greatest work of the greatest painter of antiquity, the picture by

---

[1] It is noticeable that the god three times defended his own shrine,—against Xerxes (Herod. viii. 36), Jason of Pherae (Xen. *Hell.* vi. 4), Brennus (Paus. x. 23).

Polygnotus in the Hall of the Cnidians at Delphi, of the descent of Odysseus among the dead.[1]  For as it was with the oracle of Teiresias that the roll of responses began, so it is the picture of that same scene which shows us, even through the meagre description of Pausanias, how great a space had been traversed between the horizon and the zenith of the Hellenic faith.  "The ethical painter," as Aristotle calls him,[2] the man on whose works it ennobled a city to gaze, the painter whose figures were superior to nature as the characters of Homer were greater than the greatness of men, had spent on this altar-piece, if I may so term it, of the Hellenic race his truest devotion and his utmost skill.  The world to which he introduces us is Homer's shadow-world, but it reminds us also of a very different scene.  It recalls the visions of that Sacred Field on whose walls an unknown painter has set down with so startling a reality the faith of mediæval Christendom as to death and the hereafter.

In place of Death with her vampire aspect and wiry wings, we have the fiend Eurynomus, "painted of the blue-black colour of flesh-flies," and battening

---

[1] For this picture see Paus. x. 28-31 ; also Welcker (*Kleine Schriften*), and W. W. Lloyd in the Classical Museum, who both give Riepenhausen's restoration.  While differing from much in Welcker's view of the picture, I have followed him in supposing that a vase figured in his *Alte Denkmäler*, vol. iii. plate 29, represents at any rate the figure and expression of Polygnotus' *Odysseus*. The rest of my description can, I think, be justified from Pausanias.

[2] Ar. *Pol.* viii. 8 ; *Poet.* ii. 2.

on the corpses of the slain. In place of the kings
and ladies, who tell us in the rude Pisan epigraph
how

> " Ischermo di savere e di richezza
> Di nobiltate ancora e di prodezza
> Vale niente ai colpi de costei,"—

it is Theseus and Sisyphus and Eriphyle who teach
us that might and wealth and wisdom " against
those blows are of no avail." And Tityus, whose
scarce imaginable outrage in the Pythian valley
upon the mother of Apollo herself carries back his
crime and his penalty into an immeasurable past,—
Tityus lay huge and prone upon the pictured field,
but the image of him (and whether this were by
chance or art Pausanius could not say) seemed melt-
ing into cloud and nothingness through the infinity
of his woe. But there also were heroes and heroines
of a loftier fate,—Memnon and Sarpedon, Tyro and
Penthesilea, in attitudes that told that "calm pleasures
there abide, majestic pains ;"—Achilles, with Patro-
clus at his right hand, and near Achilles Protesilaus,
fit mate in valour and in constancy for that type of
generous friendship and passionate woe. And there
was Odysseus, still a breathing man, but with no
trace of terror in his earnest and solemn gaze, de-
manding from Teiresias, as Dante from Virgil, all
that that strange world could show ; while near him
a woman's figure stood, his mother Anticleia, waiting to call to him in those words which in Homer's

song seem to strike at once to the very innermost
of all love and all regret.   And where the mediæval
painter had set hermits praying as the type of souls
made safe through their piety and their knowledge
of the divine, the Greek had told the same parable
after another fashion.   For in Polygnotus' picture
it was Tellis and Cleoboia, a young man and a maid,
who were crossing Acheron together with hearts at
peace ; and amid all those legendary heroes these
figures alone were real and true, and of a youth and
a maiden who not long since had passed away ; and
they were at peace because they had themselves
been initiated, and Cleoboia had taught the mysteries
of Demeter to her people and her father's house.
And was there, we may ask, in that great company,
any heathen form which we may liken, however
distantly, to the Figure who, throned among the
clouds on the glowing Pisan wall, marshals the
blessed to their home in light?   Almost in the
centre, as it would seem, of Polygnotus' picture was
introduced a mysterious personality who found no
place in Homer's poem,—a name round which had
grown a web of hopes and emotions which no hand
can disentangle now, — "The minstrel sire of song,
Orpheus the well-beloved, was there."

It may be that the myth of Orpheus was at
first nothing more than another version of the world-
old story of the Sun; that his descent and resurrection were but the symbols of the night and the day;

that Eurydice was but an emblem of the lovely rose-clouds which sink back from his touch into the darkness of evening only to enfold him more brightly in the dawn. But be this as it may, the name of Orpheus [1] had become the centre of the most aspiring and the deepest thoughts of Greece; the lyre which he held, the willow-tree on which in the picture his hand was laid, were symbols of mystic meaning, and he himself was the type of the man "who has descended and ascended"— who walks the earth with a heart that turns continually towards his treasure in a world unseen.

When this great picture was painted, the sanctuary and the religion of Delphi might well seem indestructible and eternal. But the name of Orpheus, introduced here perhaps for the first time into the centre of the Apolline faith, brings with it a hint of that spirit of mysticism which has acted as a solvent,—sometimes more powerful even than criticism, as the sun in the fable of Aesop was more powerful than the wind,—upon the dogmas of every religion in turn. And it suggests a forward glance to an oracle given at Delphi on a later day,[2] and cited by Porphyry to illustrate the necessary evanescence and imperfection of whatsoever image

[1] See, for instance, Maury, *Religions de la Grèce*, chap. xviii. Aelius Lampridius (*Alex. Sev. Vita*, 29) says—"In Larario et Apollonium et Christum, Abraham et Orpheum, et hujusmodi deos habebat."

[2] Eus. *Pr. Ev.* vi. 3.

of spiritual things can be made visible on earth. A
time shall come when even Delphi's mission shall
have been fulfilled; and the god himself has predicted without despair the destruction of his holiest
shrine—

> " Ay, if ye bear it, if ye endure to know
> That Delphi's self with all things gone must go,
> Hear with strong heart the unfaltering song divine
> Peal from the laurelled porch and shadowy shrine.
> High in Jove's home the battling winds are torn,
> From battling winds the bolts of Jove are born;
> These as he will on trees and towers he flings,
> And quells the heart of lions or of kings;
> A thousand crags those flying flames confound,
> A thousand navies in the deep are drowned,
> And ocean's roaring billows, cloven apart,
> Bear the bright death to Amphitrite's heart.
> And thus, even thus, on some long-destined day,
> Shall Delphi's beauty shrivel and burn away,—
> Shall Delphi's fame and fane from earth expire
> At that bright bidding of celestial fire."

The ruin has been accomplished. All is gone, save
such cyclopean walls as date from days before
Apollo, such ineffaceable memories as Nature herself
has kept of the vanished shrine.[1] Only the Cory-
cian cave still shows, with its gleaming stalagmites,
as though the nymphs to whom it was hallowed
were sleeping there yet in stone; the Phaedriades

---

[1] See Mr. Aubrey de Vere's *Picturesque Sketches in Greece and
Turkey* for a striking description of Delphian scenery. Other
details will be found in Foucart, pp. 113, 114; and cf. Paus. x. 33.

or Shining Crags still flash the sunlight from their
streams that scatter into air; and dwellers at
Castri still swear that they have heard the rushing
Thyiades keep their rout upon Parnassus' brow.

### III.

Even while Polygnotus was painting the Lesche
of the Cnidians at Delphi a man was talking in the
Athenian market-place, from whose powerful individuality, the most impressive which Greece had
ever known, were destined to flow streams of influence which should transform every department
of belief and thought. In tracing the history of
oracles we shall feel the influence of Socrates mainly
in two directions; in his assertion of a personal and
spiritual relation between man and the unseen
world, an oracle not without us but within; and in
his origination of the idea of science, of a habit of
mind which should refuse to accept any explanation
of phenomena which failed to confer the power of
predicting those phenomena or producing them anew.
We shall find that, instead of the old acceptance of
the responses as heaven-sent mysteries, and the old
demands for prophetic knowledge or for guidance in
the affairs of life, men are more and more concerned
with the questions: How can oracles be practically
produced? and what relation between God and man
do they imply? But first of all, the oracle which

concerned Socrates himself, which declared him to
be the wisest of mankind, is certainly one of the
most noticeable ever uttered at Delphi.   The fact
that the man on whom the god had bestowed this
extreme laudation, a laudation paralleled only by ~
the mythical words addressed to Lycurgus, should a
few years afterwards have been put to death for
impiety, is surely one of a deeper significance than ⌐
has been often observed.   It forms an overt and
impressive instance of that divergence between the
law and the prophets, between the letter and the
spirit, which is sure to occur in the history of all religions, and on the manner of whose settlement the
destiny of each religion in turn depends.   In this
case the conditions of the conflict are striking and
unusual.[1]   Socrates is accused of failing to honour
the gods of the State, and of introducing new gods
under the name of demons, or spirits, as we must
translate the word, since the title of demon has
acquired in the mouths of the Fathers a bad signi-
fication.   He replies that he *does* honour the gods
of the State, as he understands them, and that the
spirit who speaks with him is an agency which he
cannot disavow.

The first count of the indictment brings into
prominence an obvious defect in the Greek religion,

---

[1] On the trial of Socrates and kindred points see, besides Plato
(*Apol.*, *Phaed.*, *Euthyphr.*) and Xenophon (*Mem.*, *Apol.*), Diog.
Laert. ii. 40. Diod. Sic. xiv. 37, Plut. *De genio Socratis.*

the absence of any inspired text to which the
orthodox could refer. Homer and Hesiod, men
like ourselves, were the acknowledged authors of
the theology of Greece ; and when Homer and
Hesiod were respectfully received, but interpreted
with rationalising freedom, it was hard to know by
what canons to judge the interpreter. The second
count opens questions which go deeper still. It
was indeed true, though how far Anytus and
Meletus perceived it we cannot now know, that the
demon of Socrates indicated a recurrence to a wholly
different conception of the unseen world, a conception before which Zeus and Apollo, heaven-god and
sun-god, were one day to disappear. But who,
except Apollo himself, was to pronounce on such a
question ? It was he who was for the Hellenic
race the source of continuous revelation ; his utterances were a sanction or a condemnation from which
there was no appeal. And in this debate his verdict
for the defendant had been already given. We
have heard of Christian theologians who are " more
orthodox than the Evangelists." In this case the
Athenian jurymen showed themselves more jealous
for the gods' honour than were the gods themselves.

To us, indeed, Socrates stands as the example of
the truest religious conservatism, of the temper of
mind which is able to cast its own original convictions in an ancestral mould, and to find the last
outcome of speculation in the humility of a trustful

faith.   No man, as is well known, ever professed a
more childlike confidence in the Delphian god than
he, and many a reader through many a century has
been moved to a smile which was not far from tears
at his account of his own mixture of conscientious
belief and blank bewilderment when the infallible
deity pronounced that Socrates was the wisest of
mankind.

A spirit balanced like that of Socrates could
hardly recur; and the impulse given to philosophical
inquiry was certain to lead to many questionings as
to the true authority of the Delphic precepts.   But
before we enter upon such controversies, let us trace
through some further phases the influence of the
oracles on public and private life.

For it does not appear that Delphi ceased to give
utterances on the public affairs of Greece so long as
Greece had public affairs worthy the notice of a god.
Oracles occur, with a less natural look than when
we met them in Herodotus, inserted as a kind of
unearthly evidence in the speeches of Aeschines and
Demosthenes.[1]   Hyperides confidently recommends
his audience to check the account which a messenger
had brought of an oracle of Amphiaraus by despatch-
ing another messenger with the same question to
Delphi.[2]   Oracles, as we are informed, foretold the

---

[1] *e.g.* Dem. *Meid.* 53 :—τῷ δήμῳ τῶν Ἀθηναίων ὁ τοῦ Διὸς σημαίνει,
etc.

[2] Hyper. *Euxen.* p. 8.

battle of Leuctra,[1] the battle of Chaeronea,[2] the destruction of Thebes by Alexander.[3] Alexander himself consulted Zeus Ammon not only on his own parentage but as to the sources of the Nile, and an ingenuous author regrets that, instead of seeking information on this purely geographical problem, which divided with Homer's birthplace the curiosity of antiquity, Alexander did not employ his prestige and his opportunities to get the question of the origin of evil set at rest for ever.[4]  We hear of oracles given to Epaminondas,[5] to the orator Calli-stratus,[6] and to Philip of Macedon.[7]  To Cicero the god gave advice which that sensitive statesman would have done well to follow,—to take his own character and not the opinion of the multitude as his guide in life.[8]

Nero, too, consulted the Delphian oracle, which pleased him by telling him to "beware of seventy-three,"[9] for he supposed that he was to reign till he reached that year.  The god, however, alluded to the age of his successor Galba.  Afterwards Nero,—grown to an overweening presumption which could brook no rival worship, and become, as we may say, Antapollo as well as Antichrist,—murdered certain men and cast them into the cleft of Delphi, thus

---

[1] Paus. ix. 14.     [2] Plut. *Dem.* 19.     [3] Diod. xvii. 10.
[4] Max. Tyr. *Diss.* 25.  [5] Paus. viii. 11.  [6] Lycurg. *Leocr.* 160.
[7] Diod. xvi. 91.
[8] Plut. *Cic.* 5.                [9] Suet. *Nero*, 38.

extinguishing for a time the oracular power.[1]
Plutarch, who was a contemporary of Nero's,
describes in several essays this lowest point of
oracular fortunes.  Not Delphi alone, but the great
majority of Greek oracles, were at that time hushed,
a silence' which Plutarch ascribes partly to the
tranquillity and depopulation of Greece, partly to a
casual deficiency of Demons,—the immanent spirits
who give inspiration to the shrines, but who are
themselves liable to change of circumstances, or
even to death.[2]

Whatever may have been the cause of this
oracular eclipse, it was of no long duration.  The
oracle of Delphi seems to have been restored in the
reign of Trajan; and in Hadrian's days a characteristic
story shows that it had again become a centre of
distant inquirers.  The main preoccupation of that
imperial scholar was the determination of Homer's
birthplace, and he put the question in person to the
Pythian priestess.  The question had naturally been
asked before, and an old reply, purporting to have
been given to Homer himself, had already been
engraved on Homer's statue in the sacred precinct. —

[1] Dio Cass. lxiii. 14.  Suetonius and Dio Cassius do not know
why Nero destroyed Delphi; but some such view as that given in
the text seems the only conceivable one.

[2] Plut. *de Defect. orac.* 11.  We may compare the way in which
Heliogabalus put an end to the oracle of the celestial goddess of the
Carthaginians, by insisting on marrying her statue, on the ground
that she was the Moon and he was the Sun.—Herodian, v. 6.

But on the inquiry of the sumptuous emperor the priestess changed her tone, described Homer as "an immortal siren," and very handsomely made him out to be the grandson both of Nestor and of Odysseus.[1] It was Hadrian, too, who dropped a laurel-leaf at Antioch into Daphne's stream, and when he drew it out there was writ thereon a promise of his imperial power. He choked up the fountain, that no man might draw from its prophecy such a hope again.[2] But Hadrian's strangest achievement was to found an oracle himself. The worshippers of Antinous at Antinoe were taught to expect answers from the deified boy: "They imagine," says the scornful Origen, "that there breathes from Antinous a breath divine."[3]

For some time after Hadrian we hear little of Delphi. But, on the other hand, stories of oracles of varied character come to us from all parts of the Roman world. The bull Apis, "trampling the unshowered grass with lowings loud," refused food from the hand of Germanicus, and thus predicted his approaching death.[4] Germanicus, too, drew the same dark presage from the oracle at Colophon of the Clarian Apollo.[5] And few oracular answers have

---

[1] Anth. Pal. xiv. 102 :—ἄγνωστον μ' ἐρέεις γενεῆς καὶ πατρίδος αἴης ἀμβροσίου Σειρῆνος, etc.

[2] Sozomen, *Hist. Eccl.* v. 19.

[3] Orig. *ad. Cels.* ap. Wolff, *de Noviss.* p. 43, where see other citations.

[4] Plin. viii. 46.   [5] Tac. *Ann.* ii. 54.

been more impressively recounted than that which
was given to Vespasian by the god Carmel, upon
Carmel, while the Roman's dreams of empire were
still hidden in his heart. "Whatsoever it be, Vespasian, that thou preparest now, whether to build
a house or to enlarge thy fields, or to get thee servants for thy need, there is given unto thee a mighty
home, and far-reaching borders, and a multitude of
men."[1]

The same strange mingling of classic and Hebrew
memories, which the name of Carmel in this connection suggests, meets us when we find the god Bel at
Apamea,—that same Baal "by whom the prophets
prophesied and walked after things that do not
profit" in Jeremiah's day,—answering a Roman
emperor in words drawn from Homer's song. For
it was thus that the struggling Macrinus received
the signal of his last and irretrievable defeat:[2]—

"Ah, king outworn! young warriors press thee sore,
　And age is on thee, and thou thyself no more."

In the private oracles, too, of these post-classical
times there is sometimes a touch of romance which
reminds us how much human emotion there has

---

[1] Tac. *Hist.* ii. 78. Suetonius, *Vesp.* 5, speaks of Carmel's *oracle*,
though it seems that the answer was given after a simple *extispi-
cium.*

[2] Dio Cass. lxxviii 40 ; Hom. *Il.* viii. 103. Capitolinus, in his
life of Macrinus (c. 3), shows incidentally that under the Antonines
it was customary for the Roman proconsul of Africa to consult the
oracle of the Dea Caelestis Carthaginiensium.

been in generations which we pass rapidly by; how earnest and great a thing many a man's mission has seemed to him, which to us is merged in the dulness and littleness of a declining age. There is something of this pathos in the Pythia's message to the wandering preacher,[1] "Do as thou now doest, until thou reach the end of the world," and in the dream which came to the weary statesman in Apollo Grannus' shrine,[2] and bade him write at the end of his life's long labour Homer's words—

"But Hector Zeus took forth and bare him far
From dust, and dying, and the storm of war."

And in the records of these last centuries of paganism we notice that the established oracles, the orthodox forms of inquiry, are no longer enough to satisfy the eagerness of men. In that upheaval of the human spirit which bore to the surface so much of falsehood and so much of truth,—the religion of Mithra, the religion of Serapis, the religion of Christ,—questions are asked from whatever source, glimpses are sought through whatsoever in nature has been deemed transparent to the influences of an encompassing Power. It was in this age[3] that at

[1] Dio Chrysostom, περὶ φυγῆς, p. 255. This message had, perhaps, a political meaning.

[2] Dio Cassius, ad fin.; Hom. Il. xi. 163.

[3] The following examples of later oracles are not precisely synchronous. They illustrate the character of a long period, and the date at which we happen to hear of each has depended largely on accident.

Hierapolis the " clear round stone of the onyx kind,"
which Damascius describes, showed in its mirroring
depths letters which changed and came, or sometimes emitted that "thin and thrilling sound,"[1]
which was interpreted into the message of a slowly-
uttering Power.    It was in this age that Chosroes
drew his divinations from the flickering of an eternal
fire.[2]    It was in this age that the luminous meteor
would fall from the temple of Uranian Venus upon
Lebanon into her sacred lake beneath, and declare
her presence and promise her consenting grace.[3]    It
was in this age that sealed letters containing num-
bered questions were sent to the temple of the sun
at Hierapolis, and answers were returned in order,
while the seals remained still intact.[4]    It was in
this age that the famous oracle which predicted the
death of Valens was obtained by certain men who
sat round a table and noted letters of the alphabet

[1] Damasc. ap. Phot. 348, φωνὴν λεπτοῦ σιρίσματος. See also
Paus. vii. 21, and compare Spartian, *Did. Jul.* 7, where a child sees
the images in a mirror applied to the top of his head rendered
abnormally sensitive by an unexplained process.

[2] Procop. *Bell. Pers.* ii. 24. The practice of divining from
sacrificial flame or smoke was of course an old one, though rarely
connected with any regular seat of oracle. Cf. Herod. viii. 134.
The πυρεῖον in the χωρίον 'Αδιαρβιγάνων, which Chosroes consulted,
was a fire worshipped in itself, and sought for oracular purposes.

[3] Zosimus, *Ann.* i. 57.

[4] Macrob. *Sat.* i. 23. Fontenelle's criticism (*Histoire des Oracles*)
on the answer given to Trajan is worth reading along with the
passage of Macrobius as an example of Voltairian mockery, equally
incisive and unjust. Cf. Amm. Marcell. xiv. 7 for a variety of
this form of response.

which were spelt out for them by some automatic
agency, after a fashion which, from the description
of Ammianus we cannot precisely determine.[1]　This
oracle, construed into a menace against a Christian
Emperor, gave rise to a persecution of paganism of
so severe a character that, inasmuch as philosophers
were believed especially to affect the forbidden
practice, the very repute or aspect of a philosopher,
as Sozomen tells us,[2] was enough to bring a man
under the notice of the police.　This theological
rancour will the less surprise us, if we believe with
some modern criticism that St. Paul himself, under
the pseudonym of Simon Magus, had not escaped
the charge, at the hands of a polemical Father, of
causing the furniture of his house to move without
contact, in obedience to his unholy will.[3]

Finally, to conclude this strange list with an
example which may by many minds be considered
as typical of the rest, it was in this age that, at the
Nymphaeum at Apollonia in Epirus, an Ignis Fatuus[4]
gave by its waving approach and recession the re-

---

[1] Amm. Marcell. xxix. 2, and xxxi. 1.

[2] Sozomen. vi. 35.

[3] Pseudo-Clemens, *Homil.* ii. 32. 638, τὰ ἐν οἰκίᾳ σκεύη ὡς αὐτό-
ματα φερόμενα πρὸς ὑπηρεσίαν βλέπεσθαι ποιεῖ.　Cf. Renan, *Les
Apôtres*, p. 153, note, etc.

[4] There can, I think, be little doubt that such was the true character of the flame which Dio Cassius (xli. 45) describes: πρὸς δὲ τὰς
ἐπιχύσεις τῶν ὄμβρων ἐπαύξει καὶ ἐς ὕψος ἐξαίρεται, etc.　Maury's explanation (ii. 446) is slightly different.　The fluctuations of the flame
on Etna (Paus. iii. 23) were an instance of a common volcanic
phenomenon.

sponses which a credulous people sought,—except
that this Will-o'-the-Wisp, with unexpected diffi-
dence, refused to answer questions which had to do
with marriage or with death.

Further examples are not needed to prove what
the express statement of Tertullian and others tes-
tifies,[1] that the world was still "crowded with
oracles" in the first centuries of our era. We must
now retrace our steps and inquire with what eyes
the post-Socratic philosophers[2] regarded a phenomenon so opposed to ordinary notions of enlightenment or progress.

Plato's theory of inspiration is too vast and far-
reaching for discussion here. It must be enough to
say that, although oracles seemed to him to consti-
tute but a small part of the revelation offered by
God to man, he yet maintained to the full their
utility, and appeared to assume their truth. In his

[1] Tertullian, de Anima, 46 : Nam et oraculis hoc genus stipatus
est orbis, etc. Cf. Plin. Hist. Nat. viii. 29 : Nec non et hodie mul-
tifariam ab oraculis medicina petitur. Pliny's oracular remedy for
hydrophobia (viii. 42) is not now pharmacopœal.

[2] For a good account of pre-Socratic views on this topic, see
Bouché-Leclerq, i. 29. But the fragments of the early sages tan-
talise even more than they instruct. A genuine page of Pythagoras
would here be beyond price. But it is the singular fate of the original Ipse of our Ipse Dixit that while the fact of his having said
anything is proverbially conclusive as to its truth we have no trust-
worthy means of knowing what he really did say. Later ages
depict him as the representative of continuous inward inspiration,
—as a spirit linked with the Past, the Future, the Unseen, by a
vision which is presence and a commerce which is identity.

ideal polity the oracles of the Delphian god were to
possess as high an authority, and to be as frequently
consulted, as in conservative Lacedæmon, and the
express decision of heaven was to be invoked in
matters of practical[1] as well as of ceremonial[2] import.

Aristotle, who possessed, — and no man had a
better right to it, — a religion all his own, and to
which he never converted anybody, delivered himself on the subject of oracular dreams with all his
sagacious ambiguity. "It is neither easy," he said,
"to despise such things, nor yet to believe them."[3]

The schools of philosophy which were dominant
in Greece after the death of Aristotle occupied
themselves only in a secondary way with the question of oracles. The Stoics and Academics were
disposed to uphold their validity on conservative
principles, utilising them as the most moral part of
the old creed, the point from which its junction
with philosophy was most easily made. Cicero's
treatise on divination contains a summary of the
conservative view, and it is to be remarked that
Cratippus and other Peripatetics disavowed the
grosser forms of divination, and believed only in
dreams and in the utterances of inspired frenzy.[4]

[1] *Leges*, vi. 914.     [2] *Leges*, v. 428 ; *Epinomis*, 362.
[3] Ar. *Div. per Som.* i. 1. He goes on to suggest that dreams,
though not θεόπεμπτα, may be δαιμόνια. Elsewhere he hints that
the soul may draw her knowledge of the future from her own true
nature, which she resumes in sleep. See reff. ap. Bouché-Leclercq,
i. 55.     [4] See Cic. *de Div.* i. 3.

Epicureans and Cynics, on the other hand, felt
no such need of maintaining connection with the
ancient orthodoxy, and allowed free play to their
wit in dealing with the oracular tradition, or even
considered it as a duty to disembarrass mankind of
this among other superstitions.   The sceptic Lucian
is perhaps of too purely mocking a temper to allow
us to ascribe to him much earnestness of purpose
in the amusing burlesques[1] in which he depicts the
difficulty which Apollo feels in composing his
official hexameters, or his annoyance at being
obliged to hurry to his post of inspiration whenever
the priestess chooses "to chew the bay-leaf and
drink of the sacred spring."[2]

The indignation of Oenomaus, a cynic of Hadrian's age, is of a more genuine character, and there

---

[1] *Jupiter Tragoedus; Bis Accusatus*, etc.   I need not remind
the reader that such scoffing treatment of oracles does not now
appear for the first time.   The parodies in Aristophanes hit off
the pompous oracular obscurity as happily as Lucian's.   A recent
German writer, on the other hand (Hoffmann, *Orakelwesen*), maintains, by precept and example, that no style can be more appropriate to serious topics.

[2] *Bis Accusatus*, 2.   I may remark that although narcotics are
often used to produce abnormal utterance (Lane's *Egyptians*, ii. 33 ;
Maury, ii. 479), this mastication of a laurel-leaf or bay-leaf cannot
be considered as more than a symbolical survival of such a practice.
See, however, *Proceedings* of the Society for Psychical Research,
vol. iv. p. 152, note, for a most remarkable effect of laurel-water on
a hysterical subject.   The drinking of water (Iambl. *Myst. Aeg.*
72 ; Anacreon xiii.), or even of blood (Paus. ii. 24), would be
equally inoperative for occult purposes ; and though Pliny says
that the water in Apollo's cave at Colophon shortened the drinker's

is much sarcastic humour in his account of his own
visit to the oracle of Apollo at Colophon; how the
first response which he obtained might have been
taken at random from a book of elegant extracts,
and had also, to his great disgust, been delivered in
the self-same words to a commercial traveller immediately before him; how, to his second question,
"Who will teach me wisdom?" the god returned an
answer of almost meaningless imbecility; and how,
when he finally asked, "Where shall I go now?" the
god told him "to draw a long bow and knock over
untold green-feeding ganders."[1]  "And who in the
world," exclaims the indignant philosopher, "will
inform me what these untold ganders may mean?"

Anecdotes like this may seem to warn us that
our subject is drawing to a close.  And to students
of these declining schools of Greek philosophy, it
may well appear that the Greek spirit had burnt
itself out; that all creeds and all speculations were
being enfeebled into an eclecticism or a scepticism,
both of them equally shallow and unreal.  But this
was not to be.  It was destined that every seed
which the great age of Greece had planted should
germinate and grow; and a school was now to
arise which should take hold, as it were, of the
universe by a forgotten clew, and should give fuller

---

[1] Eus. *Pr. Ev.* v. 23—

ἐκ τανυστρόφοιο λᾶας σφενδόνης ἱεὶς ἀνὴρ
χῆνας ἐναρίζειν βολαῖσιν, ἀσπέτους, ποιηβόρους.

meaning and wider acceptance to some of the most
remarkable, though hitherto least noticed, utterances
of earlier men. We must go back as far as Hesiod
to understand the Neoplatonists.

For it is in Hesiod's celebrated story of the Ages
of the World[1] that we find the first Greek conception, obscure though its details be,—of a hierarchy of spiritual beings who fill the unseen world,
and can discern and influence our own. The souls
of heroes, he says, become happy spirits who dwell
aloof from our sorrow; the souls of men of the
golden age become good and guardian spirits, who
flit over the earth and watch the just and unjust
deeds of men; and the souls of men of the silver
age become an inferior class of spirits, themselves
mortal, yet deserving honour from mankind.[2] The
same strain of thought appears in Thales, who defines demons as spiritual existences, heroes, as the
souls of men separated from the body.[3] Pythagoras
held much the same view, and, as we shall see below,
believed that in a certain sense these spirits were
occasionally to be seen or felt.[4] Heraclitus held
" that all things were full of souls and spirits,"[5] and

[1] Hes. *Opp.* 109, *sqq.*

[2] It is uncertain where Hesiod places the abode of this class
of spirits; the MSS. read ἐπιχθόνιοι, Gaisford (with Tzetzes) and
Wolff, *de Daemonibus*, ὑποχθόνιοι.

[3] Athenag. *Legat. pro Christo*, 21; cf. Plut. *de Plac. Phil.* i. 8.

[4] Porph. *vit. Pyth.* 384; reff. ap. Wolff. For obsession, see
Pseudo-Zaleucus, ap. Stob. *Flor.* xliv. 20.

[5] Diog. Laert. ix. 6.

Empedocles has described in lines of startling power[1] the wanderings through the universe of a lost and homeless soul. Lastly, Plato, in the *Epinomis*,[2] brings these theories into direct connection with our subject by asserting that some of these spirits can read the minds of living men, and are still liable to be grieved by our wrong-doing,[3] while many of them appear to us in sleep by visions, and are made known by voices and oracles, in our health or sickness, and are about us at our dying hour. Some are even visible occasionally in waking reality, and then again disappear, and cause perplexity by their obscure self-manifestation.[4]

Opinions like these, existing in a corner of the vast structure of Platonic thought, passed, as it seems, for centuries with little notice. Almost as unnoticed was the gradual development of the creed known as Orphic, which seems to have begun with making itself master of the ancient mysteries, and

[1] Plut. *de Iside*, 26.

[2] I believe, with Grote, etc., that the *Epinomis* is Plato's; at any rate it was generally accepted as such in antiquity, which is enough for the present purpose.

[3] *Epinomis*, 361. ʹμετέχοντα δὲ φρονήσεως θαυμαστῆς, ἅτε γένους ὄντα εὐμαθοῦς τε καὶ μνήμονος, γιγνώσκειν μὲν ξύμπασαν τὴν ἡμετέραν αὐτὰ διάνοιαν λέγωμεν, καὶ τόν τε καλὸν ἡμῶν καὶ ἀγαθὸν ἅμα θαυμαστῶς ἀσπάζεσθαι καὶ τὸν σφόδρα κακὸν μισεῖν, ἅτε λύπης μετέχοντα ἤδη, κ.τ.λ.

[4] καὶ τοῦτʹ εἶναι τότε μὲν ὁρώμενον ἄλλοτε δὲ ἀποκρυφθὲν ἄδηλον γιγνόμενον, θαῦμα κατʹ ἀμυδρὰν ὄψιν παρεχόμενον. The precise meaning of ἀμυδρὰ ὄψις is not clear without further knowledge of the phenomena which Plato had in his mind. Comp. the ἀλαμπῆ καὶ ἀμυδρὰν ζωήν, ὥσπερ ἀναθυμίασιν, which is all that reincarnated demons can look for (Plut. *de Defect*. 10).

only slowly spread through the profane world its
doctrine that this life is a purgation, that this body
is a sepulchre,[1] and that the Divinity, who sur-
rounds us like an ocean, is the hope and home of
the soul.    But a time came when, under the impulse of a great religious movement, these currents
of belief, which had so long run underground, broke
into sight again in an unlooked-for direction.   These
tenets, and many more, were dwelt upon and ex-
panded with new conviction by that remarkable
series of men who furnish to the history of Greek
thought so singular a concluding chapter.    And
no part, perhaps, of the Neoplatonic system shows
more clearly than their treatment of oracles how
profound a change the Greek religion has undergone
beneath all its apparent continuity.   It so happens
that the Neoplatonic philosopher who has written
most on our present subject, was also a man whose
spiritual history affords a striking, perhaps an
unique, epitome of the several stages through which
the faith of Greece had up to that time passed.   A
Syrian of noble descent,[2] powerful intelligence, and

---

[1] See, for instance, Plato, *Crat.* 264. δοκοῦσι μέντοι μοι μάλιστα
θέσθαι οἱ ἀμφὶ Ὀρφέα τοῦτο ὄνομα (σῶμα *quasi* σῆμα) ὡς δίκην
διδούσης τῆς ψυχῆς ὧν δὴ ἕνεκα δίδωσι, κ.τ.λ

[2] G. Wolff, *Porph. de Phil.* etc., has collected a mass of authorities on Porphyry's life, and has ably discussed the sequence of his
writings.   But beyond this tract I have found hardly anything
written on this part of my subject,—on which I have dwelt the
more fully, inasmuch as it seems hitherto to have attracted so little
attention from scholars.

upright character, Porphyry brought to the study of the Greek religion little that was distinctively Semitic, unless we so term the ardour of his religious impulses, and his profound conviction that the one thing needful for man lay in the truest knowledge attainable as to his relation to the divine. Educated by Longinus, the last representative of expiring classicism, the Syrian youth absorbed all, and probably more than all, his master's faith. Homer became to him what the Bible was to Luther; and he spent some years in producing the most perfect edition of the *Iliad* and *Odyssey* which had yet appeared, in order that no fragment of the inspired text might fail to render its full meaning. But, as it seems, in the performance of this task his faith received the same shock which had been fatal to the early piety of Greece. The behaviour of the gods in Homer was too bad to be condoned. He discerned, what is probably the truth, that there must be some explanation of these enormities which is not visible on the surface, and that nothing short of some profound mistake could claim acceptance for such legends as those of Zeus and Kronos, of Kronos and Uranus, amid so much else that is majestic and pure.[1] Many philologists would answer

---

[1] The impossibility of extracting a spiritual religion from Homer is characteristically expressed by Proclus (*ad. Tim.* 20), who calls Homer ἀπάθειάν τε νοεράν καὶ ζωὴν φιλόσοφον οὐχ οἶός τε παραδοῦναι.

now that the mistake, the disease of language, lay
in the expression in terms of human appetite and
passion of the impersonal sequences of the great
phenomena of Nature ; that the most monstrous
tales of mythology mean nothing worse or more
surprising than that day follows night, and night
again succeeds to day.    To Porphyry such explanations were of course impossible.    In default of
Sanskrit he betook himself to allegory.    The truth
which must be somewhere in Homer, but which
plainly was not in the natural sense of the words,
must therefore be discoverable in a non-natural
sense.    The cave of the nymphs, for instance, which
Homer describes as in Ithaca, is not in Ithaca.
Homer must, therefore, have meant by the cave
something quite other than a cave ; must have
meant, in fact, to signify by its inside the temporary, by its outside the eternal world.    But this
stage in Porphyry's development was not of long
duration.  As his conscience had revolted from Homer
taken literally, so his intelligence revolted from
such a fashion of interpretation as this.    But yet
he was not prepared to abandon the Greek religion.    That religion, he thought, must possess some
authority, some sacred book, some standard of faith,
capable of being brought into harmony with the
philosophy which, equally with the religion itself,
was the tradition and inheritance of the race.    And
such a rule of faith, if to be found anywhere, must

be found in the direct communications of the gods
to men.  Scattered and fragmentary though these
were, it must be possible to extract from them a
consistent system.[1]   This is what he endeavoured
to do in his work, *On the Philosophy to be drawn
from Oracles,* a book of which large fragments remain
to us imbedded in Eusebius' treatise *On the Preparation for the Gospel.*

Perhaps the best guarantee of the good faith in
which Porphyry undertook this task lies in the fact
that he afterwards recognised that he had been unsuccessful.  He acknowledged, in terms on which
his antagonist Eusebius has gladly seized, that the
mystery as to the authors of the responses was too
profound, the responses themselves were too unsatisfactory, to admit of the construction from them of
a definite and lofty faith.   Yet there is one point on
which, though his inferences undergo much modification, his testimony remains practically the same.[2]
This testimony, based, as he implies and his biographers assert, on personal experience,[3] is mainly
concerned with the phenomena of possession or inspiration by an unseen power.   These phenomena,

---

[1] ὡς ἂν ἐκ μόνου βεβαίου τὰς ἐλπίδας τοῦ σωθῆναι ἀρυόμενος (Eus.
*Pr. Ev.* iv. 6) is the strong expression which Porphyry gives to his
sense of the importance of this inquiry.

[2] There is one sentence in the epistle to Anebo which would
suggest a contrary view, but the later *De Abstinentia,* etc., seem to
me to justify the statement in the text.

[3] See, for instance, Eus. *Pr. Ev.* iv. 6: μάλιστα γὰρ φιλοσόφων
οὗτος τῶν καθ' ἡμᾶς δοκεῖ καὶ δαίμοσι καὶ οἷς φησι θεοῖς ὡμιληκέναι.

so deeply involved in the conception of oracles, and
which we must now discuss, are familiar to the
ethnologist in almost every region of the globe.
The savage, readily investing any unusual or striking object in nature with a spirit of its own, is
likely to suppose further that a spirit's temporary
presence may be the cause of any unusual act or
condition of a human being.   Even so slight an
abnormality as the act of sneezing has generally
been held to indicate the operation or the invasion
of a god.   And when we come to graver departures
from ordinary well-being—nightmare, consumption,
epilepsy, or madness—the notion that a disease-
spirit has entered the sufferer becomes more and
more obvious.   Ravings which possess no applicability to surrounding facts are naturally held to be
the utterances of some remote intelligence.   Such
ravings, when they have once become an object of
reverence, may be artificially reproduced by drugs
or other stimuli, and we may thus arrive at the
belief in inspiration by an easy road.[1]

There are traces in Greece of something of this
reverence for disease, but they are faint and few;
and the Greek ideal of soundness in mind and body,
the Greek reverence for beauty and strength, seem
to have characterised the race from a very early

---

[1] On this subject see *Prim. Cult.* chap. xiv.; Lubbock, *Origin
of Civilisation*, pp. 252-5, etc.   The Homeric phrase στυγερὸς δέ οἱ
ἔχραε δαίμων (*Od.* v. 396) seems to be the Greek expression which
comes nearest to the doctrine of disease-spirits.

period.   It is possible indeed that the first tradition of

> "Blind Thamyris and blind Mæonides,
> And Teiresias and Phineus, prophets old,"

may have represented a primitive idea that the
"celestial light shone inward" when the orbs of
vision were darkened.    But the legends which have
reached us scarcely connect Homer's blindness with
his song, and ascribe the three prophets' loss of
sight to their own vanity or imprudence.    In
nymph-possession, which, in spite of Pausanias'
statement, is perhaps an older phenomenon than
Apolline possession, we find delirium honoured, but
it is a delirium proceeding rather from the inhala-
tion of noxious vapours than from actual disease.[1]
And in the choice of the Pythian priestess—while
we find that care is taken that no complication shall
be introduced into the process of oracular inquiry
by her youth or good looks,[2]—there is little evidence to show that any preference was given to
epileptics.[3]   Still less can we trace any such reason

[1] See Maury, ii. 475.  Nymph-oracles were especially common
in Bœotia, where there were many caves and springs.—Paus. ix.
2, etc.  The passage from Hippocrates, *De Morbo Sacro*, cited by
Maury, ii. 470, is interesting from its precise parallelism with
savage beliefs, but cannot be pressed as an authority for primitive
tradition.

[2] Diod. Sic. xvi. 27.

[3] Maury (ii. 514) cites Plut. *de Defect. orac.* 46, and *Schol. Ar.
Plut.* 39, in defence of the view that a hysterical subject was chosen
as Pythia.  But Plutarch expressly says (*de Defect.* 50) that it was
necessary that the Pythia should be free from perturbation when

of choice in other oracular sanctuaries. We find here, in fact, the same uncertainty which hangs over the principle of selection of the god's mouthpiece in other shahmanistic countries, where the medicine-man or angekok is sometimes described as haggard and nervous, sometimes as in no way distinguish-able from his less gifted neighbours.

Nor, on the other hand, do we find in Greece much trace of that other kind of possession of which the Hebrew prophets are our great example, where a peculiar loftiness of mind and character seem to point the prophet out as a fitting exponent of the will of heaven, and a sudden impulse gives vent in words, almost unconscious, to thoughts which seem no less than divine. The majestic picture of Am-phiaraus in the Seven against Thebes, the tragic personality of Cassandra in the Agamemnon, are the nearest parallels which Greece offers to an Elijah or a Jeremiah.[1]  These, however, are mythi-

---

called on to prophesy, and the Scholion on Aristophanes is equally indecent and unphysiological. Moreover, Plutarch speaks of the custom of pouring cold water over the priestess in order to ascer-tain by her healthy way of shuddering that she was sound in body and mind. This same test was applied to goats, etc., when about to be sacrificed. There is no doubt evidence (cf. Maury, ii. 461) that the faculty of divination was supposed to be hereditary in certain families (perhaps even in certain localities, Herod. i. 78), but I cannot find that members of such families were sought for as priests in oracular seats.

[1] The exclamation of Helen (*Od.* xv. 172)—

κλῦτέ μευ, αὐτὰρ ἐγὼ μαντεύσομαι, ὡς ἐνὶ θυμῷ
ἀθάνατοι βάλλουσι καὶ ὡς τελέεσθαι ὀίω—

cal characters; and so little was the gift of prophecy associated with moral greatness in later days, that while Plato attributes it to the action of the divinity, Aristotle feels at liberty to refer it to bile.[1]

It were much to be wished that some systematic discussion of the subject had reached us from classical times. But none seems to have been composed, at any rate none has come down to us, till Plutarch's inquiry as to the causes of the general cessation of oracles in his age.[2] Plutarch's temper is conservative and orthodox, but we find, nevertheless, that he has begun to doubt whether Apollo is in every case the inspiring spirit. On the contrary, he thinks that sometimes this is plainly not the case, as in one instance where the Pythia, forced to prophesy while under the possession of a dumb and evil spirit, went into convulsions and soon afterwards died. And he recurs to a doctrine, rendered orthodox, as we have already seen, by its appearance in Hesiod, but little dwelt on in classical times, a doctrine which peoples the invisible world with a hierarchy of spirits of differing character and power. These spirits, he believes, give oracles, whose cha-

is as it were a naïve introduction to the art of prophecy. Menelaus, when appealed to as to the meaning of the portent observed, is perplexed: the more confident Helen volunteers an explanation, and impassioned rhetoric melts into inspired prediction.

[1] Plat. *Ion.* 5.—Ar. *Probl.* xxx.—I cannot dwell here on Plat. *Phaedr.* 153, and similar passages, which suggest a theory of inspiration which would carry us far beyond the present topic.

[2] Plut. *de Defect. orac.; de Pyth.; de El apud Delphos.*

racter therefore varies with the character and condition of the inspiring spirit; and of this it is hard
to judge except inferentially, since spirits are apt to
assume the names of gods on whom they in some
way depend, though they may by no means resemble
them in character or power.　Nay, spirits are not
necessarily immortal, and the death of a resident
spirit may have the effect of closing an oracular
shrine.　The death of Pan himself was announced
by a flying voice to Thamus, a sailor, "about the
isles Echinades;" he was told to tell it at Palodes,
and when the ship reached Palodes there was a
dead calm.　He cried out that Pan was dead, and
there was a wailing in all the air.[1]

In Plutarch, too, we perceive a growing disposi-
tion to dwell on a class of manifestations of which
we have heard little since Homer's time,—evocations
of the visible spirits of the dead.[2]　Certain places,
it seems, were consecrated by immemorial belief to
this solemn ceremony.　At Cumae,[3] at Phigalea,[4] at
Heraclea,[5] on the river Acheron, by the lake Aver-

[1] This quasi-human character of Pan (Herod. ii. 146 ; Pind. *Fr.*
68 ; Hyg. *Fab.* 224), coupled with the indefinite majesty which his
name suggested, seems to have been very impressive to the later
Greeks.　An oracle quoted by Porphyry (ap. Eus. *Pr. Ev.*) εὔχομαι
βροτὸς γεγὼς Πανὶ σύμφυτος θεῷ κ.τ.λ., is curiously parallel to some
Christian hymns in its triumphant sense of human kinship with
the divinity.

[2] *Quaest. Rom. ; de Defect. Orac. ; de Ser. Num. Vind.*

[3] Diod. Sic. iv. 22 ; Ephor. ap. Strab. v. 244.

[4] Paus. iii. 17.　　　　　　　　　[5] Plut. *Cim.* 6.

nus,[1] men strove to recall for a moment the souls
who had passed away, sometimes, as Periander
sought Melissa,[2] in need of the accustomed wifely
counsel; sometimes, as Pausanias sought Cleonice,[3]
goaded by passionate remorse; or sometimes with
no care to question, with no need to confess or
to be forgiven, but as, in one form of the legend,
Orpheus sought Eurydice,[4] travelling to the Thesprotian Aornus, in the hope that her spirit would rise
and look on him once again, and waiting for one
who came not, and dying in a vain appeal.

But on such stories as these Plutarch will not
dogmatically judge; he remarks only, and the remark was more novel then than now, that we know
as yet no limit to the communications of soul with
soul.

This transitional position of Plutarch may prepare us for the still wider divergence from ancient
orthodoxy which we find in Porphyry.    Porphyry
is indeed anxious to claim for oracular utterances as
high an authority as possible; and he continues to
ascribe many of them to Apollo himself.    But he
no longer restricts the phenomena of possession and
inspiration within the traditional limits as regards
either their time, their place, or their author.    He
maintains that these phenomena may be reproduced

---

[1] Liv. xxiv. 12, etc.    The origin of this νεκυομαντεῖον was probably Greek.    See reff. ap. Maury, ii. 467.

[2] Diod. iv. 22; Herod. v. 92, gives a rather different story.

[3] Plut. *Cim.* 6.  Paus. iii. 17.          [4] Paus. ix. 30.

according to certain rules at almost any place and
time, and that the spirits who cause them are of very
multifarious character. I shall give his view at
some length, as it forms by far the most careful inquiry into the nature of Greek oracles which has
come down to us from an age in which they existed
still; and it happens also that while the grace of
Plutarch's style has made his essays on the same
subject familiar to all, the post-classical date and
style of Porphyry and Eusebius have prevented their
more serious treatises from attracting much attention
from English scholars.

According to Porphyry, then, the oracular or
communicating demon or spirit,—we must adopt
spirit as the word of wider meaning,—manifests
himself in several ways. Sometimes he speaks
through the mouth of the entranced " recipient,"[1]
sometimes he shows himself in an immaterial, or
even in a material form, apparently according to
his own rank in the invisible world.[2] The recipient

---

[1] δοχεὺς, from δέχομαι, is the word generally used for the human
intermediary between the god or spirit and the inquirers. See Lob.
*Agl.* p. 108, on the corresponding word καταβολικός for the spirit
who is thus received for a time into a human being's organism.
Cf. also Firmicus Maternus *De errore prof. relig.* 13 : " Serapis
vocatus et intra corpus hominis conlatus talia respondit ; " and the
phrase ἐγκατοχήσας τῷ Σαράπιδι (*Inscr. Smyrn.* 3163, ap. Wolff,
*de Nov.*)

[2] Porphyry calls these inferior spirits δαιμόνια ὑλικά, and Proclus
(*ad Tim.* 142) defines the distinction thus : τῶν δαιμόνων οἱ μὲν ἐν τῇ
συστάσει πλέον τὸ πύριον ἔχοντες ὁρατοὶ ὄντες οὐδὲν ἔχουσιν ἀντιτύπως,
οἱ δὲ καὶ γῆς μετειληφότες ὑποπίπτουσι τῇ ἁφῇ. It is only the spirits

falls into a state of trance, mixed sometimes with
exhausting agitation or struggle,[1] as in the case of
the Pythia.    And the importance attached to a
right choice of time and circumstances for the in-
duction of this trance reminds us of Plutarch's
story, already mentioned, of the death of a Pythian
priestess compelled to prophesy when possessed by
an evil spirit.    Another inconvenience in choosing
a wrong time seems to have been that false answers
were then given by the spirit, who, however, would
warn the auditors that he could not give information,[2] or even that he would certainly tell falsehoods,[3]
on that particular occasion.    Porphyry attributes
this occasional falsity to some defect in the surrounding conditions,[4] which confuses the spirit, and pre-
vents him from speaking truly.    For on descending
into our atmosphere the spirits become subject to
the laws and influences which rule mankind, and

who partake of earthly nature who are capable of being touched.
These spirits may be of a rank inferior to mankind ; Proclus, *ad
Tim.* 24, calls them ψυχὰς ἀποτύχουσας μὲν τοῦ ἀνθρωπικοῦ νοῦ, πρὸς
δὲ τὰ ζῷα ἐχούσας διάθεσιν.

[1] οὐ φέρει με τοῦ δοχῆος ἡ τάλαινα καρδία (Procl. *ad Rempubli-
cam*, 380) is the exclamation of a spirit whose recipient can no
longer sustain his presence.

[2] Eus. *Pr. Ev.* vi. 5, σήμερον οὐκ ἐπέοικε λέγειν ἄστρων ὁδοὶ
ἱρήν.

[3] *Ibid.* κλεῖε βίην κάρτος τε λόγων· ψευδήγορα λέξω : "Try no
longer to enchain me with your words ; I shall tell you falsehoods."

[4] ἡ κατάστασις τοῦ περιέχοντος.    Eus. *Pr. Ev.* iv. 5, καὶ τὸ
περιέχον ἀναγκάζον ψευδῆ γίνεσθαι τὰ μαντεῖα, οὐ τοὺς παρόντας
ἑκόντας προστιθέναι τὸ ψεῦδος. . . . πέφηνεν ἄρα, adds Porphyry
with satisfaction, πόθεν πολλάκις τὸ ψεῦδος συνίσταται.

are not therefore entirely free agents.[1] When a
confusion of this kind occurs, the prudent inquirer
should defer his researches,—a rule with which in-
experienced investigators fail to comply.[2]

Let us suppose, however, that a favourable day
has been secured, and also, not less important, a
"guileless intermediary."[3] Some confined space
would then be selected for the expected manifestations, "so that the influence should not be too widely
diffused."[4] This place seems sometimes to have
been made dark, — a circumstance which has not
escaped the satire of the Christian controversialist,[5]
whose derision is still further excited by the "barbarous yells and singing"[6] with which the unseen
visitant was allured,—a characteristic, it may be
noticed in passing, of shahmanistic practices, where-
ever they have been found to prevail. During
these proceedings the human agent appears to have

---

[1] Porph. ap. Philoponum, de Mundi Creat. iv. 20, with the com-
ments of Philoponus, whose main objection to these theories lies
in their interference with the freedom of the will.

[2] Pr. Ev. vi. 5, οἱ δὲ μένουσι καὶ λέγειν ἀναγκάζουσι διὰ τὴν
ἀμαθίαν.

[3] Ibid. v. 8, κάππεσεν ἀμφὶ κάρηνον ἀμωμήτοιο δοχῆος.

[4] καὶ ἅμα ἀποστηρίζοντες αὐτὸ ἐνταῦθα ἔν τινι στερέῳ χωρίῳ ὥστε
μὴ ἐπιπολὺ διαχεῖσθαι, Iamb. de Myst. iii. 14. The maxims of
Iamblichus in these matters are in complete conformity with those
of Porphyry.

[5] Eus. Pr. Ev. iv. 1, καὶ τὸ σκότος δὲ οὐ μικρὰ συνεργεῖν τῇ καθ'
ἑαυτοὺς ὑποθέσει.

[6] Ibid. v. 12, ἀσήμοις τε καὶ βαρβάροις ἤχοις τε καὶ φωναῖς
κηλούμενοι.

fallen into an abnormal slumber, which extinguished
for the time his own identity, and allowed the spirit
to speak through his lips,—" to contrive a voice for
himself through a mortal instrument."[1]  In such
speeches, of which several are preserved to us, the
informing spirit alludes to the human being through
whom he is speaking in the third person, as " the
mortal " or " the recipient ;" of himself he speaks in
the first person, or occasionally in the third person,
as " the god " or " the king."[2]

The controlling spirits do not, however, always
content themselves with this vicarious utterance.
They appear sometimes, as already indicated, in
visible and tangible form.  Of this phase of the
proceedings, however, Eusebius has preserved to us
but scanty notices.  His mind is preoccupied with
the presumption and *bizarrerie* of the spirits, who
sometimes profess themselves to be (for instance)
the sun and moon; sometimes insist on being called
by barbarous names, and talking a barbarous jargon.[3]
The precise nature of such appearances had been, it
seems, in dispute since the days of Pythagoras, who
conjectured that the apparition was an emanation from
the spirit, but not, strictly speaking, the spirit itself.[4]

---

[1] *Ibid.* v. 8 αὐλοῦ δ᾽ ἐκ βροτέοιο φίλην ἐτεκνώσατο φωνήν.

[2] φῶς, βροτός, δοχεύς.  *Pr. Ev.* v. 9, λύετε λοιπὸν ἄνακτα, βροτὸς
θεὸν οὐκέτι χωρεῖ.

[3] *Pr. Ev.* v. 10 (quoting Porph. *ad Aneb.*), τί δὲ καὶ τὰ ἄσημα
βούλεται ὀνόματα καὶ τῶν ἀσήμων τὰ βάρβαρα πρὸ τῶν ἑκάστῳ
οἰκείων, etc.

[4] Pythag. ap. Aen. Gaz. ap. Theophr. p. 61, Boisson. πότερον

In the Neoplatonic view, these spirits entered by
a process of "introduction"[1] into a material body
temporarily prepared for them; or sometimes it was
said that "the pure flame was compressed into a
sacred Form."[2] Those spirits who had already been
accustomed to appear were best instructed as to how
to appear again; but some of them were inclined to
mischief, especially if the persons present showed a
careless temper.[3]

θεοὶ ἢ δαίμονες ἢ τούτων ἀπόῤῥοιαι, καὶ πότερον δαίμων εἰς ἄλλος εἶναι
δοκῶν ἢ πολλοὶ καὶ σφῶν αὐτῶν διαφέροντες, οἱ μὲν ἥμεροι, οἱ δ' ἄγριοι,
καὶ οἱ μὲν ἐνίοτε τἀληθῆ λέγοντες οἱ δ' ὅλως κίβδηλοι . . . . τέλος
προΐεται δαίμονος ἀπόῤῥοιαν εἶναι τὸ φάσμα.

[1] εἴσκρισις. See Lob. Agl. p. 730.
[2] Pr. Ev. v. 8 :—    ἱεροῖσι τύποις
                συνθλιβομένου πυρὸς ἁγνοῦ.

I may just notice here the connection between this idea of the
entrance of a spirit into a quasi-human form built up for the occasion, and that recrudescence of idol-worship which marks one phase
of Neoplatonism.  In an age when such primitive practices as
"carrying the dried corpse of a parent round the fields that he
might see the state of the crops" (Spencer's *Sociology*, § 154), were
no longer possible, this new method of giving temporary materiality
to disembodied intelligences suggested afresh that it might be prac-
ticable so to prepare an image as that a spirit would be content to
live there permanently.  An oracle in Pausanias (ix. 38) curiously
illustrates this view of statues.  The land of the Orchomenians was
infested by a spirit which sat on a stone.  The Pythia ordered them
to make a brazen image of the spectre and fasten it with iron to
the stone.  The spirit would still be there, but he would now be
permanently fixed down, and, being enclosed in a statue, he would
no longer form an obnoxious spectacle.

[3] Pr. Ev. v. 8, ἔθος ποιησάμενοι τῆς ἑαυτῶν παρουσίας εὐμαθέστερον
φοιτῶσι καὶ μάλιστα ἐὰν καὶ φύσει ἀγαθοὶ τυγχάνωσιν, οἱ δὲ, κἂν ἔθος
ἔχωσι τοῦ παραγίνεσθαι, βλάβην τινὰ προθυμοῦνται ποιεῖν, καὶ μάλιστα
ἐὰν ἀμελέστερόν τις δοκῇ ἀναστρέφεσθαι ἐν τοῖς πράγμασι.  This notion

After a time the spirit becomes anxious to depart;
but is not always able to quit the intermediary as
promptly as it desires.　We possess several oracles
uttered under these circumstances, and giving directions which we can but imperfectly understand.　It
appears that the recipient, for what reason we are left
to conjecture, was in some way bound with withes
and enveloped in fine linen, which had to be cut
and unwrapped at the end of the ceremony.[1]　The
human agent had then to be set on his feet and taken
from the corner where he had been outstretched, and
a singular collaboration seems to have taken place,
the spirit giving his orders to the bystanders by a
voice issuing from the recipient's still senseless form.[2]
At last the spirit departs, and the recipient is set free.

Eusebius, in a passage marked by strong common
sense,[3] has pointed out some obvious objections to
oracles obtained in this fashion.　Some of these so-

of a congruity between the inquirer and the responding spirit is
curiously illustrated by a story of Caracalla (Dio Cass. lxxvii.), who
ἐψυχαγώγησε μὲν ἄλλας τέ τινας καὶ τὴν τοῦ πατρὸς τοῦ τε Κομμόδου
ψυχήν· εἶπε δ' οὖν οὐδεὶς αὐτῷ οὐδὲν, πλὴν τοῦ Κομμόδου. Ἔφη γὰρ
ταῦτα· βαῖνε δίκης ἆσσον, θεοὶ ἦν αἰτοῦσι Σεβήρῳ.　No ghost would
address Caracalla except the ghost of Commodus, who spoke to
him his doom.

[1] Pr. Ev. v. 8:—παύεο δὴ περίφρων ὀάρων, ἀνάπαυε δὲ φῶτα,
θάμνων ἐκλύων πολιὸν τύπον, ἠδ' ἀπὸ γυίων
Νειλαίην ἐθόνην χερσὶν στιβαρῶς ἀπάειρας.
And again, when the bystanders delay the release, the spirit
exclaims—　σίνδονος ἀμπέτασον νεφέλην, λῦσόν τε δοχῆα.

[2] Pr. Ev. v. 8 ;—ὑψίπρωρον αἶρε ταρσὸν, ἴσχε βάξιν ἐκ μυχῶν. And
again, ἄρατε φῶτα γαίηθεν ἀναστήσαντες ἑταῖροι, etc.

[3] Pr. Ev. iv. 2.

called " recipients," it appears, had been put to the torture and had made damaging confessions. Further penalties had induced them to explain how their fraud was carried out. The darkness and secrecy of the proceedings were in any case suspicious; and the futility of many of the answers obtained, or their evident adaptation to the wishes of the inquirers, pointed too plainly to their human origin. The actual method of producing certain phenomena has exercised the ingenuity of other Fathers. Thus figures could be shown in a bowl of water by using a moveable bottom, or lights could be made to fly about in a dark room by releasing a vulture with flaming tow tied to its claws.[1]

But in spite of these contemptuous criticisms the Christian Fathers, as is well known, were disposed to believe in the genuineness of some at least of these communications, and showed much anxiety to induce the oracles, which often admitted the greatness and wisdom, to acknowledge also the divinity, of Christ.[2]

Eusebius himself, in another work,[3] adduces a letter of Constantine's describing an oracle said to have been uttered directly by Apollo " from a certain dark hole," in which the god asserted that he could no longer speak the truth on account of

[1] Pseudo-Origen, *Philosophumena*, p. 73.
[2] *Pr. Ev.* iv. iii. 7. Aug. *de Civit. Dei*, xix. 23. Lact. *Instit.* iv. 13.
[3] *Vit. Const.* ii. 50; cf. Wolff, *de Noviss.* p. 4.

the number of saints who were now on the earth.
But this has so little the air of an Apolline manifestation that it is suspected that a Christian man
had crept into a cave and delivered this unauthor-
ised response with a polemical object.[1]

Into so obscure, so undignified a region of mingled
fraud and mystery does it seem that, by the admission of friends and foes alike, the oracles of Greece
had by this time fallen.   Compared with what had
been stripped away, that which was left may seem
to us like the narrow vault of the Delian sanctuary
compared with the ruined glories of that temple-
covered isle.   There was not, indeed, in Porphyry's
view anything inconsistent with the occasional presence and counsel of a lofty and a guardian spirit.
There was nothing which need make him doubt
that the Greeks had been led upwards through their
long history by some providential power.   Nay, he
himself cites, as we shall see, recent oracles higher
in tone than any which have preceded them.   Yet
as compared with the early ardour of that imaginative belief which peopled heaven with gods and
earth with heroes, we feel that we are now sent
back to " beggarly elements ;" that the task of sift-
ing truth from falsehood amid so much deception
and incompetency on the part both of visible and

---

1 The well-known story, Γρηγόριος τῷ Σατανᾷ Εἴσελθε—Greg.
Nyss. 548 (and to be found in all lives of Gregory Thaumaturgus),
illustrates this Christian rivalry with pagan oracles or apparitions.

invisible agencies,[1] of erecting a consistent creed on
such mean and shifting foundations, might well
rebut even the patient ardour of this most untiring
of "seekers after God." And when we see him recognising all this with painful clearness, giving vent,
in that letter to Anebo which is so striking an
example of absolute candour in an unscrupulous
and polemic age, to his despair at the obscurity
which seems to deepen as he proceeds, we cannot but
wonder that we do not see him turn to take refuge in
the new religion with its offers of certainty and peace.

Why, we shall often ask, should men so much
in earnest as the Neoplatonists have taken, with the
gospel before them, the side they took? Why
should they have preferred to infuse another allegory into the old myths which had endured so
much? to force the Pythian Apollo, so simple-
hearted through all his official ambiguity, to strain
his hexameters into the ineffable yearnings of a
theosophic age? For we seem to see the issues so
clearly! when we take up Augustine instead of
Proclus we feel so instantly that we have changed to
the winning side! But to Greek minds—and the glory
of the Syrian Porphyry was that, of all barbarians,
he became the most intensely Greek—the struggle

---

[1] The disappointing falsity of the manifesting spirits who pre-
tended to be the souls of departed friends, etc., is often alluded to ;
*e.g.* in the *ad Anebonem*: οἱ δὲ εἶναι μὲν ἔξωθεν τίθενται τὸ ὑπήκοον
γένος ἀπατηλῆς φύσεως, παντόμορφόν τε καὶ πολύτροπον, ὑποκρινόμενον
καὶ θεοὺς καὶ δαίμονας καὶ ψυχὰς τεθνηκότων, etc.

presented itself in a very different fashion. They were fighting not for an effete mythology, but for the whole Past of Greece; nay, as it seemed in a certain sense, for the civilisation of the world. The repulse of Xerxes had stirred in the Greeks the consciousness of their uniqueness as compared with the barbarism on every side. And now, when Hellenism was visibly dying away, there awoke in the remaining Greeks a still more momentous conception, the conception of the uniqueness and preciousness of Greek life not only in space but in duration, as compared not only with its barbarian compeers, but with the probable future of the world. It was no longer against the Great King, but against Time itself, that the unequal battle must be waged. And while Time's impersonal touch was slowly laid upon all the glory which had been, a more personal foe was seen advancing from the same East from whose onset Greece had already escaped, "but so as by fire." Christ, like Xerxes, came against the Greek spirit Συριήγενες ἅρμα διώκων, driving a Syrian car; the tide of conquest was rolling back again, and the East was claiming an empire such as the West had never won.

We, indeed, knowing all the flower of European Christianity in Dante's age, all its ripening fruit in our own, may see that this time from the East light came; we may trust and claim that we are living now among the scattered forerunners of

such types of beauty and of goodness as Athens
never knew.   But if so much even of our own
ideal is in the future still, how must it have been to
those whose longest outlook could not overpass the
dreary centuries of barbarism and decay ?   So vast
a spiritual revolution must needs bring to souls of
differing temper very different fates.   Happy were
they who, like Augustine and Origen, could frankly
desert the old things and rejoice that all things
were become new.   Happy, too, were those few
saintly souls—an Antoninus or a Plotinus—whose
lofty calm no spiritual revolution seemed able to
reach or mar.   But the pathetic destiny was that
of men like Julian or Porphyry, men who were dis-
qualified from leading the race onward into a noble
future merely because they so well knew and loved
an only less noble past.

And yet it is not for long that we can take
Porphyry as an example of a man wandering in the
twilight between "dying lights and dawning," between an outworn and an untried faith.   The last
chapter in the history of oracles is strangely connected with the last stage of the spiritual history of
this upward-striving man.

For it was now that Porphyry was to encounter
an influence, a doctrine, an aim, more enchanting
than Homer's mythology, profounder than Apollo's
oracles, more Christian, I had almost written, than
Christianity itself.   More Christian at least than

such Christianity as had chiefly met Porphyry's eyes; more Christian than the violence of bishops, the wrangles of heretics, the fanaticism of slaves, was that single-hearted and endless effort after the union of the soul with God which filled every moment of the life of Plotinus, and which gave to his living example a potency and a charm which his writings never can renew.[1] "Without father, without mother, without descent," a figure appearing solitary as Melchisedek on the scene of history, charged with a single blessing and lost in the unknown, we may yet see in this chief of mystics the heir of Plato, and affirm that it is he who has completed the cycle of Greek civilisation by adding to that long gallery of types of artist and warrior, philosopher and poet, the stainless image of the saint.

It may be that the holiness which he aimed at is not for man. It may be that ecstasy comes best unsought, and that the still small voice is heard seldomer in the silence of the wilderness than through the thunder of human toil and amid human passion's fire.

But those were days of untried capacities, of unbounded hopes. In the Neoplatonist lecture-

---

[1] Eunapius (vit. Porph.) manages to touch the heart, in spite of his affectations, when he describes the friendship between Porphyry and Plotinus. Of Porphyry's first visit to Rome he says :—τὴν μεγίστην Ῥώμην ἰδεῖν ἐπιθυμήσας . . . ἐπειδὴ τάχιστα εἰς αὐτὴν ἀφίκετο καὶ τῷ μεγίστῳ Πλωτίνῳ συνῆλθεν εἰς ὁμιλίαν, πάντων ἐπελάθετο τῶν ἄλλων, κ.τ.λ.

room, as at the Christian love-feast, it seemed that
religion had no need to compromise, that all this
complex human spirit could be absorbed and trans-
figured in one desire.

Counsels of perfection are the aliment of strenuous souls, and henceforth, in each successive book of
Porphyry's, we see him rising higher, resting more
confidently in those joys and aspirations which are
the heritage of all high religions, and the substance
of the communion of saints.

And gradually, as he dwells more habitually in
the thought of the supreme and ineffable Deity, the
idea of a visible or tangible communion with any
Being less august becomes repugnant to his mind.
For what purpose should he draw to him those
unknown intelligences from the ocean of environing
souls? "For on those things which he desires to
know there is no prophet nor diviner who can
declare to him the truth, but himself only, by communion with God, who is enshrined indeed in his
heart."[1]  "By a sacred silence we do Him honour,
and by pure thoughts of what He is."[2]  "Holding
Him fast, and being made like unto Him, let us
present ourselves, a holy sacrifice, for our offering
unto God."[3]

---

[1] *De Abstin.* ii. 54.

[2] *Ibid.* ii. 34, διὰ δὲ σιγῆς καθαρᾶς καὶ τῶν περὶ αὐτοῦ καθαρῶν
ἐννοιῶν θρησκεύομεν αὐτῷ.

[3] *Ibid.* ii. 34, δεῖ ἄρα συναφθέντας καὶ ὁμοιωθέντας αὐτῷ τὴν αὐτῶν
αναγωγὴν θυσίαν ἱερὰν πϙοσαγαγεῖν τῳ θεῷ.

And in his letter to the well-loved wife of his old age,—than which we find no higher expression of the true Platonic love (so often degraded and misnamed)—no nobler charge and counsel of man to woman in all the stores which antiquity has bequeathed,— in this last utterance we find him risen above all doubt and controversy, and rapt in the contemplation of that Being whom " no prayers can move and no sacrifice honour, nor the abundance of offerings find favour in His sight; only the inspired thought fixed firmly on Him has cognisance of God indeed."[1]   It may seem that as we enter on this region we have left oracles behind. But it is not so.   The two last oracles which I shall cite, and which are among the most remarkable of all, are closely connected with this last period of Porphyry's life.   The first of them is found, by no chance we may be sure, on a leaf of the manuscript which contains his letter to Marcella.   It is introduced to us by an unknown writer as " an oracle concerning the Eternal God."[2]

[1] τὸ ἔνθεον φρόνημα καλῶς ἡδρασμένον συνάπτεται τῷ θεῷ.—See the *Ad Marcellam* passim.

[2] This oracle was very probably actually delivered in a shrine, as the utterances of this period were often tinged with Neoplatonism. I have followed Wolff's emendations, and must refer the reader to his *Porph. Fragm.* p. 144, and especially his *Addit. IV. de Daemonibus*, p. 225, in support of the substantial accuracy of my rendering. It is impossible to reproduce all the theology which this hymn contains ; I have tried to bring out the force of the most central and weighty expressions, such as ἀενάοις ὀχετοῖσι τιθηνῶν νοῦν ἀτάλαντον. The oracle will also be found in Steuchus, *de Perenni Philosophia*,

"O God ineffable, eternal Sire,
Throned on the whirling spheres, the astral fire,
Hid in whose heart thy whole creation lies,—
The whole world's wonder mirrored in thine eyes,—
List thou thy children's voice, who draw anear,
Thou hast begotten us, thou too must hear!
Each life thy life her Fount, her Ocean knows,
Fed while it fosters, filling as it flows;
Wrapt in thy light the star-set cycles roll,
And worlds within thee stir into a soul;
But stars and souls shall keep their watch and way,
Nor change the going of thy lonely day.

   Some sons of thine, our Father, King of kings,
Rest in the sheen and shelter of thy wings,—
Some to strange hearts the unspoken message bear,
Sped on thy strength through the haunts and homes of
     air,—
Some where thine honour dwelleth hope and wait,
Sigh for thy courts and gather at thy gate;
These from afar to thee their praises bring,
Of thee, albeit they have not seen thee, sing;
Of thee the Father wise, the Mother mild,
Thee in all children the eternal Child,
Thee the first Number and harmonious Whole,
Form in all forms, and of all souls the Soul."

The second oracle above alluded to, the last which
I shall quote, was given, as Porphyry tells us, at
Delphi to his friend Amelius, who inquired, "Where
was now Plotinus' soul?"[1]

iii. 14; Orelli, *Opusc. gr. vett. sentent.* i. 319; and Mai's edition of
the *Ad Marcellam.*

  [1] Porph. *vit. Plot.* 22. It is seldom that the genuineness of an

Whatever be the source of this poem, it stands out to us as one of the most earnest utterances of antiquity, though it has little of classical perfection of form. Nowhere, indeed, is the contest more apparent between the intensity of the emotions which are struggling for utterance and the narrow limits of human speech, which was composed to deal with the things that are known and visible, and not with those that are inconceivable and unseen.

Little, in truth, it is which the author of this oracle could express, less which the translator can render; but there is enough to show once more the potency of an elect soul, what a train of light she may leave behind her as she departs on her unknown way; when for those who have lived in her presence, but can scarcely mourn her translation, the rapture of love fades into the rapture of worship. Plotinus was "the eagle soaring above the tomb of Plato;" no wonder that the eyes which followed his flight must soon be blinded with the sun.

"Pure spirit—once a man—pure spirits now
　　Greet thee rejoicing, and of these art thou;

oracle can be established on grounds which would satisfy the critical historian. But this oracle has better external evidence than most others. Of Porphyry's own good faith there is no question, and though we know less of the character of his fellow-philosopher Amelius, it seems unlikely that he would have wished to deceive Porphyry on an occasion so solemn as the death of their beloved master, or even that he could have deceived him as to so considerable an undertaking as a journey to Delphi.

Not vainly was thy whole soul alway bent
With one same battle and one the same intent
Through eddying cloud and earth's bewildering roar
To win her bright way to that stainless shore.
Ay, 'mid the salt spume of this troublous sea,
This death in life, this sick perplexity,
Oft on thy struggle through the obscure unrest
A revelation opened from the Blest—
Showed close at hand the goal thy hope would win,
Heaven's kingdom round thee and thy God within.[1]
So sure a help the eternal Guardians gave,
From life's confusion so were strong to save,
Upheld thy wandering steps that sought the day
And set them steadfast on the heavenly way.
Nor quite even here on thy broad brows was shed
The sleep which shrouds the living, who are dead ;
Once by God's grace was from thine eyes unfurled
This veil that screens the immense and whirling world,
Once, while the spheres around thee in music ran,
Was very Beauty manifest to man ;—
Ah, once to have seen her, once to have known her there,
For speech too sweet, for earth too heavenly fair !
But now the tomb where long thy soul had lain
Bursts, and thy tabernacle is rent in twain ;
Now from about thee, in thy new home above,
Has perished all but life, and all but love,—
And on all lives and on all loves outpoured
Free grace and full, a Spirit from the Lord,

---

[1] ἐφάνη γοῦν τῷ Πλωτίνῳ σκοπὸς ἐγγύθι ναίων· τέλος γὰρ αὐτῷ καὶ σκοπὸς ἦν τὸ ἐνωθῆναι καὶ πελάσαι τῷ ἐπὶ πᾶσι θεῷ. Ἔτυχε δὲ τετράκις που, ὅτε συνήμην αὐτῷ, τοῦ σκοποῦ τούτου ἐνεργείᾳ ἀρρήτῳ καὶ οὐ δυνάμει.—(Porph. *vit. Plot.*)

High in that heaven whose windless vaults enfold
Just men made perfect, and an age all gold.
Thine own Pythagoras is with thee there,
And sacred Plato in that sacred air,
And whoso followed, and all high hearts that knew
In death's despite what deathless Love can do.
To God's right hand they have scaled the starry way—
Pure spirits these, thy spirit pure as they.
Ah saint ! how many and many an anguish past,
To how fair haven art thou come at last !
On thy meek head what Powers their blessing pour,
Filled full with life, and rich for evermore ! "

This, so far as we know, was the last utterance
of the Pythian priestess. Once more, indeed, a
century afterwards, a voice was heard at Delphi.
But that voice seems rather to have been, in
Plutarch's phrase, "a cry floating of itself over
solitary places," than the deliverance of any recognised priestess, or from any abiding shrine. For
no shrine was standing more. The words which
answered the Emperor Julian's search were but the
whisper of desolation, the last and loveliest expression of a sanctity that had passed away. A strange
coincidence ! that from that Delphian valley, whence,
as the legend ran, had sounded the first of all hexameters,[1]—the call, as in the childhood of the world,
to "birds to bring their feathers and bees their
wax " to build by Castaly the nest-like habitation

---

[1] ξυμφέρετε πτερά τ' οἰωνοὶ κηρόν τε μέλιτται.—Plut. de Pyth.
xvii.; and reff. ap. Hendess, Orac. Graec. p. 36.

of the young new-entering god, — from that same
ruined place where " to earth had fallen the glorious
dwelling," from the dry channel where " the water-
springs that spake were quenched and dead," —
should issue in unknown fashion the last fragment
of Greek poetry which has moved the hearts of
men, the last Greek hexameters which retain the
ancient cadence, the majestic melancholy flow !¹

Stranger still, and of deeper meaning, is the fate
which has ordained that Delphi, born with the
birth of Greece, symbolising in her teaching such
light and truth as the ancient world might know,
silenced once only in her long career, and silenced
not by Christ, but by Antichrist, should have proclaimed in her last triumphant oracle the canonisa-
tion of the last of the Greeks, should have responded
with her last sigh and echo to the appeal of the
last of the Romans.

And here I shall leave the story of Greek
oracles.  It may be, indeed, that some strange and
solitary divinities—the god Jaribolus at Palmyra,²
the god Marnas at Gaza,³ the god Besa at

---

¹ εἴπατε τῷ βασιλῆι, χαμαὶ πέσε δαίδαλος αὐλά·
    οὐκέτι Φοῖβος ἔχει καλύβαν, οὐ μάντιδα δάφνην,
    οὐ παγὰν λαλέουσαν· ἀπέσβετο καὶ λάλον ὕδωρ.
—Ge. Cedren. *Hist. Comp.* i. 304 ; and see Mr. Swinburne's poem,
"The Last Oracle."

² *Inscr. Gr.* 4483 ap. Wolff, *de Noviss.* p. 27.  There is, however, no proof of Jaribolian utterance later than A.D. 242.

³ Marc. Diac. *vit. Porph. Episc.* ap. *Acta Sanctorum*, and Wolff,
*de Noviss.* p. 26.  Circ. A.D. 400.

Abydos[1]—still uttered from time to time some perishing prophecy, some despairing protest against the new victorious faith.    But that such oracles there still were is proved rather from Christian legislation than from heathen records.    On these laws I will not dwell, nor recount how far the Christian emperors fell from their divine ideal when they punished by pillage,[2] by torture,[3] and by death[4] the poor unlearned "villagers," whose only crime it was that they still found in the faith of their fathers the substance of things hoped for, and an evidence of things not seen.    Such stains will mar the noblest revolutions, but must not blind us to the fact that a spiritual revolution follows only on a spiritual need.    The end of the Greek oracles was determined not from without, but from within. They had passed through all their stages.    Fetishism, Shahmanism, Nature-worship, Polytheism, even Monotheism and Mysticism, had found in turn a home in their immemorial shrines.    Their utterances had reflected every method in which man has

---

[1] Amm. Marc. xix. 12 (A.D. 359).

[2] *Cod. Theod.* xvi. 10 (Theodosius I.)

[3] Amm. Marc. xxi. 12 (Constantius).

[4] *Cod. Justin.* ix. 18 (Constantius); *Theod. leg. Novell.* iii. (Theodosius II.)  These laws identify paganism as far as possible with magic, and, by a singular inversion, Augustine quotes Virgil's authority (*Aen.* iv. 492) in defence of the persecution of his own faith.  See Maury, *Magie*, etc., p. 127.  The last struggle of expiring paganism was in defence of the oracular temple of Serapis at Alexandria, A.D. 389

sought communion with the Unseen, from systematic experiment to intuitive ecstasy. They had completed the cycle of their scripture from its Theogony to its Apocalypse; it was time that a stronger wave of revelation should roll over the world, and that what was best and truest in the old religion should be absorbed into and identified with the new.[1]

And if there be some who feel that the youth, the *naïveté*, the unquestioning conviction, must perish not from one religion only, but from all; that the more truly we conceive of God, the more unimaginable He becomes to us, and the more infinite, and the more withdrawn; that we can no longer " commune with Him from oak or rock as a young man communes with a maid; "—to such men the story of the many pathways by which mankind has striven to become cognisant of the Unseen may have an aspect of hope as well as of despondency.

For before we despair of a question as unanswerable we must know that it has been rightly asked. And there are problems which can become clearly

[1] I need hardly remind the reader that the Church continued till the Renaissance to believe in the reality of the Greek oracles, though condemning the " demons " who inspired them. To refer them, in fact, entirely to illusion and imposture is an argument not without danger for the advocate of any revealed religion. " Celui," says M. Bouché-Leclercq, " qui croit à la 'Providence et à l'efficacité de la prière doit se rappeler qu'il accepte tous les principes sur lesquels repose la divination antique."

defined to us only by the aid of premature and imperfect solutions.    There are many things which
we should never have known had not inquiring
men before us so often deemed vainly that they knew.

Suspense of judgment, indeed, in matters of such
moment, is so irksome an attitude of mind, that we
need not wonder if confidence of view on the one
side is met by a corresponding confidence on the
other ; if the trust felt by the mass of mankind in
the adequacy of one or other of the answers to these
problems which have been already obtained is re-
butted by the decisive assertion that all these
answers have been proved futile and that it is idle
to look for more.

Yet such was not the temper of those among
the Greeks who felt, as profoundly perhaps as we,
the darkness and the mystery of human fates.    To
them it seemed no useless or unworthy thing to
ponder on these chief concerns of man with that
patient earnestness which has unlocked so many
problems whose solution once seemed destined to
be for ever unknown.    "For thus will God," as
Sophocles says in one of those passages (*Fr.* 707)
whose high serenity seems to answer our perplexities
as well as his own—

"Thus then will God to wise men riddling show
Such hidden lore as not the wise can know ;
Fools in a moment deem his meaning plain,
His lessons lightly learn, and learn in vain."

And even now, in the face of philosophies of materialism and of negation so far more powerful than any which Sophocles had to meet, there are yet some minds into which, after all, a doubt may steal,—whether we have indeed so fully explained away the beliefs of the world's past, whether we can indeed so assuredly define the beliefs of its future,—or whether it may not still befit us to track with fresh feet the ancient mazes, to renew the world-old desire, and to set no despairing limit to the knowledge or the hopes of man.

# VIRGIL.

"Light among the vanished ages; star that gildest yet this
   phantom shore;
Golden branch amid the shadows, kings and realms that set to
   rise no more."

IN literature, as in life, affection and reverence may
reach a point which disposes to silence rather than
to praise. The same ardour of worship which
prompts to missions or to martyrdom when a saving
knowledge of the beloved object can be communi-
cated so, will shrink from all public expression
when the beauty which it reveres is such as can be
made manifest to each man only from within. A
sense of desecration mingles with the sense of incapacity in describing what is so mysterious, so
glorious, and so dear.

Perhaps the admirer may hear the object of
his reverence ignorantly misapprehended, unwisely
judged. Still he will shrink from speech; he will
be unwilling to seem to proffer his own poor and
disputable opinion on matters which lie so far above
any support which he can give. Yet, possibly, if

his admiration has notoriously been shared for nineteen centuries by all whose admiration was best
worth having, he may venture to attempt to prove
the world right where others have attempted the
bolder task of proving it mistaken; or rather, if the
matter in question be one by its very nature incapable of proof, he may without presumption restate
in terms adapted to modern readers the traditional
judgment of sixty generations of men.[1]

The set which the German criticism of this century has made against Virgil is a perfectly explicable,
and in one sense a perfectly justifiable thing. It is
one among many results which have followed from
the application of the historical faculty, pure and
simple, to the judgment of Art. Since every work
of art is a historical product, it can be used to illus-

---

[1] In writing on an author who has been so constantly discussed
for many centuries it is impossible to refer each fragment of criticism to its original source. Most of the sounder reflections on Virgil
have occurred to many minds and long ago, and form an anony-
mous—almost an œcumenical—tradition. Among modern writers
on Virgil, I have consulted Bernhardy, Boissier, Cantù, Comparetti,
Conington, Gladstone, Henry, Heyne, Keble, Long, Nettleship,
Ribbeck, Sainte-Beuve, Sellar, Teuffel, Wagner, etc.; some of
them with mere dissent and surprise, others—especially Boissier and
Conington—with great interest and profit. But next to Virgil's
own poems, I think that the Divina Commedia is the most important
aid to his right apprehension. The exquisite truth and delicacy
of Dante's conception of his great master become more and more
apparent if the works of the two are studied in connection.

Since this essay was first published, the greatest poet of our
times has offered to Virgil a crowning homage,—in accents that
recall his own.

trate the growth of the national life from which it
springs; it can be represented as the necessary
result of its epoch and its environment. The several
arts, however, offer very different facility to the
scientific historian. Music, the most unmixedly
imaginative of the arts, has baffled all efforts to
correlate her growth with the general march of
society. Painting bears a more intimate relation to
life, and in much of the preference which has been
lately shown for early *naïveté* over self-conscious
excellence we may detect a mixture of the historical
with the purely æsthetic instinct. The historic
instinct, indeed, works in admirably with the tastes
of an elaborate civilisation. For the impulse of
historic science is naturally towards the Origines or
sources of things; it seeks to track styles and
processes to their fountain-head, and to find them
exhibiting themselves without self-consciousness
or foreign admixture; it would even wish to
eliminate the idiosyncrasies of individual artists
from its generalised estimate of the genius of a
nation. And in highly-cultivated societies there is
a somewhat similar craving—a wish to escape from
all that speaks of effort or preparation, into the
refreshing simplicity of a spontaneous age. This
craving was strongly felt under the Roman Empire;
it is potent among ourselves; it is wholly natural
and innocent so long as it is not allowed to sway
us in our estimate of the highest art.

But if the historical spirit can thus modify the judgments passed upon painting, much more is this the case with regard to poetry. For poetry is the most condensed and pregnant of all historical phenomena; it is a kind of crystallised deposit of the human spirit. It is most necessary that the historian and the philologer should be allowed free range over this rich domain. And there is no doubt a sense in which poems, as they become more remote from us, are fuller of the rough reality of things. There is a sense in which the song of the Fratres Arvales is of more value than the Fourth Eclogue. And there is a sense—and this is a point on which the Germans have especially dwelt—in which the whole Latin literature of the Augustan age, whose outer form, at least, is so confessedly derived from Greek models, is of less interest than those models themselves. If we wish to understand the native type, the original essence of epic or lyric poetry, we must go to Homer and not to Virgil, to Sappho and not to Horace. Yet this test, like all sweeping and *à priori* methods of estimating works of art, requires in practice so many limitations as to be almost valueless. It is impossible to judge a literature by its originality alone, without condemning much that is best in our modern literatures more severely than we condemn the Augustan poets. Imitation is very much a matter of chronology; it may be conscious or un-

conscious,—ostentatious or concealed,—but as the
world goes on, it tends irresistibly to form a larger
and larger element in all new productions. And
yet each new production may be in essentials
superior to its type or forerunner. Its relative
merit can be determined by experience alone—can
only be judged, for instance, in the case of poetry
by the uncertain and difficult process of comparing
the amount of delight and elevation received from
each work by the consensus of duly qualified men.
For, in the face of some recent German criticism, it
seems important to repeat that in order to judge
poetry it is before all things necessary to enjoy it.
We may all desire that historical and philological
science should push her dominion into every recess
of human action and human speech. But we must
utter some protest when the very heights of Parnassus are invaded by a spirit which surely is not
Science, but her unmeaning shadow;—a spirit
which would degrade every masterpiece of human
genius into the mere pabulum of hungry professors,
and which values a poet's text only as a field for
the rivalries of sterile pedantry and arbitrary conjecture.

It is sometimes said, *àpropos* of the new unction
with which physical science has assumed the office
of the preacher, that men of the world must be
preached to either by men of the world or by saints
— not by persons, however eminent and right-

minded, whose emotions have been confined to the laboratory. There is something of a similar incongruity in the attitude of a German commentator laboriously endeavouring to throw a new light on some point of delicate feeling or poetic propriety. Thus one of them objects to Dido's " auburn tress " on the ground that a widow's hair should be of a darker colour. Another questions whether a broken heart can be properly termed " a fresh wound," if a lady has been suffering from it for more than a week. A third bitterly accuses Virgil of exaggerating the felicity of the Golden Age. And Ribbeck alters the text of Virgil, in defiance of all the manuscripts, because the poet's picture (A. xii. 55) of Amata, " self-doomed to die, clasping for the last time her impetuous son-in-law," seems to him tame and unsatisfactory. By the alteration of *moritura* into *monitura* he is able to represent Amata as clinging to Turnus, not " with the intention of killing herself," but " with the intention of giving advice," which he considers as the more impressive and fitting attitude for a mother-in-law.[1]

It seems somewhat doubtful whither this lofty *à priori* road may lead us. And yet it is impossible to criticise any form of art without the introduction

---

[1] A single instance will give an idea of Ribbeck's fitness to deal with metrical questions. In A. ix. 67, "qua temptet ratione aditus, et quae via clausos," he reads (against all the MSS.) *et qua vi clausos*, and proves at some length the elegance of his trispondaic termination.

of subjective impressions of some kind. It would
be in vain to attempt to give any such general exposition of poetical excellence as should carry conviction
to all minds. Some obvious shortcomings may be
pointed out, some obvious merits insisted on; but
when a higher region is reached we find that a
susceptibility to the specific power of poetry is no
more communicable than an ear for music. To
most readers the subtle, the unexpressed, the infinite element in poetry such as Virgil's will remain
for ever unacknowledged and unknown. Like the
golden bough which unlocked the secrets of the
underworld—

" Itself will follow, and scarce thy touch await,
    If thou be chosen, and if this be fate;
    Else for no force shalt thou its coming feel,
    Nor shear it from the stem with shattering steel."[1]

---

[1] A. vi. 146. The translations from Virgil which I have given
in this essay, though faithful to his meaning, as I apprehend it,
are not verbally exact; while, like all my predecessors, I have
failed to convey any adequate notion of his music or his dignity,
and may well fear the fate of Salmoneus, "who thought to rival
with flash of lamps and tramp of horses the inimitable thunderbolt
and storm." But to reproduce a great poet in another language is
as impossible as to reproduce Nature on canvas; and the same
controversy between a literal and an impressional rendering divides
landscape-painters and translators of poetry. In the case of an
author so complex and profound as Virgil, every student will
naturally discern a different phase of his significance, and it seems
almost a necessary element in any attempt to criticise him that
the critic should try to show the view which he takes of a few
well-known passages. Mr. Morris' brilliant and accurate version

A few general considerations, however, may at any rate serve to indicate the kinds of achievement at which Virgil aimed — the kinds of merit which are or are not to be looked for in his poems.

The range of human thoughts and emotions greatly transcends the range of such symbols as man has invented to express them; and it becomes therefore, the business of Art to use these symbols in a double way. They must be used for the direct representation of thought and feeling; but they must also be combined by so subtle an imagination as to suggest much which there is no means of directly expressing. And this can be done; for experience shows that it is possible so to arrange forms, colours, and sounds as to stimulate the imagination in a new and inexplicable way. This power makes the painter's art an imaginative as well as an imitative one; and gives birth to the art of the musician, whose symbols are hardly imitative at all, but express emotions which, till music suggests them, have been not only unknown but unimaginable. Poetry is both an imitative and an imaginative art. As a choice and condensed form of emotional speech, it possesses the reality which depends on its directly recalling our previous thoughts and feelings. But as a system of rhythmical and melodious effects — not indebted for their potency

represents a view so different from mine (though quite equally legitimate), that it would hardly have served my present purpose.

to their associated ideas alone — it appeals also
to that mysterious power by which mere arrange-
ments of sound can convey an emotion which no
one could have predicted beforehand, and which no
known laws can explain.

It is true that the limits of melody within which
poetry works are very narrow. Between an exquisite and a worthless line there is no difference
of sound in any way noticeable to an unintelligent
ear. For the mere volume of sound — the actual
sonority of the passage — is a quite subordinate
element in the effect, which is produced mainly by
relations and sequences of vowels and consonants,
too varying and delicate to be reproducible by rule,
although far more widely similar, among European
languages at least, than is commonly perceived.[1]
But this limitation of the means employed, which
may itself be an added source of pleasure from the
sense which it may give of difficulty overcome, is
by no means without analogies in other forms of
art. The poet thrills us with delight by a collo-
cation of consonants, much as the etcher suggests
infinity by a scratch of the needle.

[1] An interesting confirmation of this statement may be obtained
by reading some passage of Latin poetry first according to the
English and then according to the Italian or the revived Latin
pronunciation. The effects observed in the first case are not
altered—are merely enriched—by the transference of the vowel
sounds to another scale. But this natural music of language (if
we may so term it) is too complex a subject to be more than
touched on here.

And, indeed, in poetry of the first order, almost every word (to use a mathematical metaphor) is raised to a higher power. It continues to be an articulate sound and a logical step in the argument; but it becomes also a musical sound and a centre of emotional force. It becomes a musical sound;—that is to say, its consonants and vowels are arranged to bear a relation to the consonants and vowels near it, — a relation of which accent, quantity, rhyme, assonance, and alliteration are specialised forms, but which may be of a character more subtle than any of these. And it becomes a centre of emotional force; that is to say, the complex associations which it evokes modify the associations evoked by other words in the same passage in a way quite distinct from grammatical or logical connection. The poet, therefore, must avoid two opposite dangers. If he thinks too exclusively of the music and the colouring of his verse—of the imaginative means of suggesting thought and feeling—what he writes will lack reality and sense. But if he cares only to communicate definite thought and feeling according to the ordinary laws of eloquent speech, his verse is likely to be deficient in magical and suggestive power.

And what is meant by the vague praise so often bestowed on Virgil's unequalled style is practically this, that he has been, perhaps, more successful than any other poet in fusing together the expressed and the suggested emotion; that he has discovered the hidden music which can give to every shade of

feeling its distinction, its permanence, and its charm;
that his thoughts seem to come to us on the wings
of melodies prepared for them from the foundation
of the world.   But in treating of so airy and
abstract a matter it is well to have frequent
recourse to concrete illustration.   Before we attempt
further description of Virgil's style, or his habitual
mood of mind, let us clear our conceptions by a
careful examination of some few passages from his
poems.   As we turn the leaves of the book we find
it hard to know on what passages it were best to
dwell.   What varied memories are stirred by one
line after another as we read!   What associations
of all dates, from Virgil's own lifetime down to the
political debates of to-day!   On this line [1] the
poet's own voice faltered as he read.   At this [2]
Augustus and Octavia melted into passionate weep-
ing.   Here is the verse [3] which Augustine quotes
as typical in its majestic rhythm of all the pathos
and the glory of pagan art, from which the Christian
was bound to flee.   This is the couplet [4] which
Fénelon could never read without admiring tears.
This line Filippo Strozzi scrawled on his prison-
wall, when he slew himself to avoid worse ill. [5]
These are the words [6] which, like a trumpet-call,

[1] Hoc solum nomen quoniam de conjuge restat.   A. iv. 324.
[2] Tu Marcellus eris, etc.   A. vi. 883.
[3] Infelix simulacrum atque ipsius umbra Creusae.   A. ii. 772.
[4] Aude, hospes, contemnere opes, et te quoque dignum
     Finge deo, rebusque veni non asper egenis.   A. viii. 364.
[5] Exoriare aliquis nostris ex ossibus ultor.   A. iv. 625.
[6] Heu ! fuge crudelis terras, fuge litus avarum.   A. iii. 44

roused Savonarola to seek the things that are above.
And this line [1] Dante heard on the lips of the
Church Triumphant, at the opening of the Paradise
of God.   Here, too, are the long roll of prophecies,
sought tremblingly in the monk's secret cell, or echoing in the ears of emperors [2] from Apollo's shrine,
which have answered the appeal made by so many
an eager heart to the Virgilian Lots—that strange
invocation which has been addressed, I believe, to
Homer, Virgil, and the Bible alone; the offspring
of men's passionate desire to bring to bear on their
own lives the wisdom and the beauty which they
revered in the past, to make their prophets in such
wise as they might—

> " Speak from those lips of immemorial speech,
>      If but one word for each."

Such references might be multiplied indefinitely.
But there is not at any rate need to prove the
estimation in which Virgil has been held in the
past.   The force of that tradition would only be
weakened by specification.   " The chastest poet,"
in Bacon's words, " and royalest, Virgilius Maro,
that to the memory of man is known," has lacked
in no age until our own the concordant testimony
of the civilised world.   No poet has lain so close
to so many hearts ; no words so often as his have

[1] Manibus date lilia plenis.  A. vi. 884.
[2] Claudius, Hadrian, Severus, etc., " in templo Apollinis
Cumani."

sprung to men's lips in moments of excitement and self-revelation, from the one fierce line retained and chanted by the untameable boy who was to be Emperor of Rome,[1] to the impassioned prophecy of the great English statesman[2] as he pleaded till morning's light for the freedom of a continent of slaves.

And those who have followed by more secret ways the influence which these utterances have exercised on mankind know well, perhaps themselves have shared, the mass of emotion which has slowly gathered round certain lines of Virgil's as it has round certain texts of the Bible, till they come to us charged with more than an individual passion and with a meaning wider than their own—with the cry of the despair of all generations,[3] with the yearning of all loves unappeased,[4] with the anguish of all partings,[5] "beneath the pressure of separate eternities."

Perhaps there will be no better way of forming an intimate conception of the poet's own nature than by analysing his treatment of two or three of

---

[1] Clodius Albinus.   Arma amens capio ; nec sat rationis in armis.  A. ii. 314.

[2] Pitt.   G. i. 250.

Nosque ubi primus equis Oriens adflavit anhelis,
Illic sera rubens accendit lumina Vesper.

[3] Quo res summa loco, Panthu ? quam prendimus arcem ?  A. ii. 322.

[4] Illum absens absentem auditque videtque.  A. iv. 83.

[5] Quem fugis ? extremum fato, quod te adloquor, hoc est.  A. vi. 466.

his principal characters, and especially of his hero,
so often considered as forming the weakest element
in his poem. Æneas, no doubt, looks at once tame
and rigid beside the eager and spontaneous warriors
of the Homeric epoch, and, so far as the Æneid is
a poem of action and adventure, he is not a stirring
or an appropriate hero. But we must not forget
that there was a special difficulty in making his
character at once consistent and attractive. He is
a man who has survived his strongest passion, his
deepest sorrow ; who has seen his "Ilium settle into
flame," and from "Creusa's melancholy shade," and
the great ghost of Hector fallen in vain, has heard
the words which sum the last disaster and close
the tale of Troy. It is no fault of his that he is
left alive ; and the poem opens with the cry of his
regret that he too has not been able to fall dead
upon the Trojan plain, "where Hector lies, and huge
Sarpedon, and Simois rolls so many warriors' corses
to the sea." But it is not always at a man's
crowning moment that his destiny and his duty
close ; and for those who fain had perished with
what they held most dear, fate may reserve a more
tedious trial, and the sad triumphs of a life whose
sun has set. It is to this note that all the adven-
tures of Æneas respond. We find him when he
lands at Carthage at once absorbed in the pictures
which show the story of Priam and of his city's
fall—

" What realm of earth, he answered, doth not know,
    O friend, our sad pre-eminence of woe ?
    Tears waken tears, and honour honour brings,
    And mortal hearts are moved by mortal things." [1]

Then he himself tells that tale, with an intensity of
pathos too well known to need further allusion.
And when his story brings him to calmer scenes—
to his meeting with "Hector's Andromache" on the
Chaonian shore — those who have loved and lost
will recognise in their colloquy the touches that
paint the fond illusion of the heart which clings,
with a half smile at its own sad persistency, to the
very name and semblance of the places by love
made dear,[2] which seeks in the eyes or movements
of surviving kindred some glance or gesture of the
dead.[3]   Take one more instance only—the meeting
of Æneas with Deiphobus in the underworld—and
note how the same cry breaks from him [4] as that
with which he greeted the vision of Hector,[5] — a
cry of reverence heightened by compassion — that

---

[1] Quis jam locus, inquit, Achate,
Quae regio in terris nostri non plena laboris ?
En Priamus ! sunt hic etiam sua praemia laudi ;
Sunt lacrimae rerum, et mentem mortalia tangunt. A. i. 459.

[2] Procedo, et parvam Troiam simulataque magnis
Pergama et arentem Xanthi cognomine rivum
Adgnosco, Scaeaeque amplector limina portae.   A. iii. 349.

[3] Cape dona extrema tuorum
O mihi sola mei super Astyanactis imago !
Sic oculos, sic ille manus, sic ora ferebat ;
Et nunc aequali tecum pubesceret aevo.   A. iii. 488.

[4] A. vi. 502.            [5] A. ii. 255.

mingling of emotions which makes the utmost
ardour of worship and of love—a cry of indignation
such as rends the generous heart at the sight of an
exalted spirit on which vileness and treachery have
been allowed to work their will. How delicately
does the " anima cortese Mantovana " stand revealed
in the lofty reverence with which Æneas addresses
the maimed Deiphobus,[1] even while he " hardly
knows him, as he trembles and strives to hide his
ghastly wounds!" How strangely sweet the cadence
in which the living friend laments that he could
not see that other, as he lay in death,[2] could only
invoke his spirit with a threefold salutation, and
rear an empty tomb! In such sad converse Æneas
loses the brief time granted for his visit to the
underworld, till the Sibyl warns him that it is
being spent in vain—

> " The night is going, Trojan ; shall it go
> Lost in an aimless memory of woe?"[3]

But he does not part from his murdered friend till
he has given the assurance that all that could be
done has been done; that he has paid the utter-
most honour and satisfied the unforgetful shade.

Yet once more ; perhaps the deepest note of all
is struck when the old love is encountered by a
new, and yet both that memory and that fresh joy

---

[1] Deiphobe armipotens, genus alto a sanguine Teucri. A. vi. 500.
[2] A. vi. 507.
[3] Nox ruit, Aenea, nos flendo ducimus horas. A. vi. 539.

must give place to an over-ruling call.   When Dido
implores Æneas to remain in Carthage, after the messenger of Jove has bidden him depart, he answers in
words whose solemn movement reveals a long-un-
uttered pain, and shows that neither in Carthage,
nor yet in Italy, can his heart expect a home [1]—

> " Me had the fates allowed my woes to still,—
> Take my sad life, and shape it at my will,—
> First had I sought my buried home and joy,
> Loves unforgotten, and the last of Troy ;—
> Ay, Priam's palace had re-risen then,
> A ghost of Ilium for heart-broken men."

It is thus that the solemn appeal evokes the
unlooked-for avowal; once and for all he makes it
known that the memory which to others is growing
dim and half-forgotten in the past, is to him ever
present and ever guiding, and always and unalterably
dear.

No doubt it is probable that Virgil would have
been ill able to describe a more buoyant and adventurous hero.   No doubt it is true that such a
nature as that of Æneas is ill fitted to fill the leading *rôle* in a poem of action.   But granting that we
have him here in the wrong place, and should have
preferred a character whom the poet could not draw,
we yet surely cannot say, when we remember Æneas'
story, that the picture given of him is meaningless
or untrue; we cannot call it unnatural that we

---

[1] A. iv. 340.

should find in all his conduct something predeter-
mined, hieratic, austere; we cannot wonder if the
only occasion on which he rises to passionate excitement is where he implores the Sibyl for pity's sake
to bring him to the sight and presence of the soul
he holds so dear;[1] or if, when from that soul in
Paradise he has learnt the secrets of the dead, his
temper thenceforth is rather that of the Christian
saint than of the Pagan warrior, and he becomes the
type of those mediæval heroes, those Galahads and
Percivals, whose fiercest exploits are performed with
a certain remoteness of spirit — who look beyond
blood and victory to a concourse of unseen specta-
tors and a sanction that is not of men.

It is, however, on another character that the
personal interest of the Æneid has been generally
felt to turn.  The story of Dido has been said to
mark the dawn of romance.  It is no doubt the
case, though how far this is accidental it is hard to
say, that the ancients have dealt oftener with the
tragedies resulting from the passion of love, than
with the delineation of that passion itself.  Sappho,
in her early world, had written, as it were, the epigraph over love's temple-door in letters of fire.
Catullus had caught the laughing glory of Septimius
and Acme—of amorous girl and boy; Lucretius
had painted, with all the mastering force of Rome,
the pangs of passion baffled by its own intensity and

---

[1] A. vi. 117

festering unsated in a heart at war.   But once only,
perhaps, do we find the joy of love's appearing, the
desolation of his flight, sung of before Virgil's days
with a majesty and a pathos like his own.   No one
who has read has forgotten how " once to Ilion's
towers there seemed to come the spirit of a windless
calm—a gentle darling of wealth, soft dart of answering eyes, love's soul-subduing flower."   Few have
heard unmoved of the " semblances of mournful
dreams " which brought to that deserted husband
" an empty joy; for all in vain, when his delight he
seemed to see, forth gliding from his arms the vision
vanished far, on swift wings following the ways of
sleep."   In Æschylus, as in Virgil, the story derives
its pathos from the severing of happy loves.   In
Æschylus they are separated by the woman's mis-
doing; in Virgil by a higher obligation which the
man is bidden to fulfil, yet an obligation which the
woman bitterly denies, and which we are ourselves
half unwilling to allow.   Neither of these plots is
quite satisfactory.   For in the atmosphere of noble
poetry we cannot readily endure that love should
either be marred by sin or unreconciled with duty;
and no cause of lovers' separation is in harmony with
our highest mood, unless it be the touch of death,
whose power is but a momentary thing, or so high a
call of honour as can give to the parting death's promise and not only his pain.

The power with which Dido is drawn is unques-

tionable.   Her transitions of feeling, her ardent
soliloquies, reveal a dramatic force in Virgil of a very
unexpected kind—an insight into the female heart
which is seldom gained by the exercise of imagination alone.   But when we compare the Fourth
Æneid with later poems on the same lofty level—
with the *Vita Nuova*, for instance, or with *Laodamia*
—we feel how far our whole conception of woman-
hood has advanced since Virgil's day under the
influence of Christianity, chivalry, civilisation.   A
nature like Dido's will now repel as much as it
attracts us.   For we have learnt that a woman may
be childlike as well as impassioned, and soft as well
as strong; that she may glow with all love's fire
and yet be delicately obedient to the lightest whisper
of honour.   The most characteristic factor in Dido's
story is of a more external kind.   It is the contrast
between the queen's stately majesty and the subduing power of love which is most effectively used
to intensify the dramatic situation.   And the picture
suggests a few reflections as to the way in which the
wealth and magnificence of Roman society affected
the poets of the age.

It happens that three great Latin poets, in strik-.
ingly similar passages,[1] have drawn the contrast
between a simple and a splendid life.   Horace, here,
as elsewhere, shows himself the ideal poet of society;
more cultivated, sensitive, affectionate than the men

---

[1] Lucr. ii. 24.   Virg. G. ii. 468.   Hor. Carm. iii. 1, 41.

and women among whom he moves, yet not so far
above them or aloof from them but that he can
delight, even more keenly than they, in their luxury
and splendour — can enjoy it without envy, as he
can dispense with it without regret.    Lucretius is
the aristocrat with a mission; to him the lamp-
bearing images, and the blaze of midnight banquets,
and the harp that echoes beneath the ceiling's fretted
gold—all these are but a vain and bitter jest which
cannot drive superstition from the soul, nor kill those
fears of death which "mingle unabashed amongst
kings and kesars," awed not at all by golden glitter
or by purple sheen.    Virgil is the rustic of genius,
well educated, of delicately refined nature, wholly
free from base admirations or desires, but "reared
amid the woods and copses," and retaining to the
last some touch of shyness in the presence of this
world's grandeur; ever eager to escape from the
palace-halls into his realm of solitude and song.
The well-known passage in the Georgics depicts, as
we may well imagine, in its vein of dignified irony,
his own sensations when he mixed with the society
which so eagerly sought him at Rome.    We have
his embarrassment at the crowd of visitors coming
and going as he calls on Pollio or Mæcenas at the
fashionable hour of 7 A.M.; his ennui as he ac-
companies over the house a party of virtuosi, open-
mouthed at the æsthetic furniture; and even his
disgust at the uncomfortable magnificence of his

bedchamber, and at the scented oil which is served
to him with his salad at dinner.[1]    And what a
soaring change when from the stately metrical roll
which reflects the pomp and luxury of the imperial
city, he mounts without an effort into that airy rush
which blends together all "the glory of the divine
country," its caverns, and its living lakes, and haunts
of wild things in the glade, its "life that never dis-
appoints," its life-long affections, and its faith in
God![2]

Yet Virgil's familiarity with the statelier life of
Rome was not unfruitful.    It has given to him in his
Æneid an added touch of dignity, as of one who has
seen face to face such greatness as earth can offer,
and paints without misgiving the commerce of
potentates and kings.    And thus it is that he has
filled every scene of Dido's story with a sense of
royal scope and unchartered power; as of an existence where all honours are secure already, and all
else that is wished for won, only the heart demands
an inner sanctuary, and life's magnificence still lacks
its crowning joy.    First we have the banquet, when
love is as yet unacknowledged and unknown, but
the "signs of his coming and sounds of his feet"

[1] Si non ingentem foribus domus alta superbis
Mane salutantum totis vomit aedibus undam,
Nec varios inhiant pulchra testudine postis,
Inlusasque auro vestes, Ephyreiaque æra,
Alba neque Assyrio fucatur lana veneno,   .
Nec casia liquidi corrumpitur usus olivi.   G. ii. 461.
[2] G. ii. 473.

have begun to raise all things to an intenser glow;
when the singer's song rises more glorious, and all
voices ring more full and free,[1] and ancestral ceremonies are kindled into life by the ungovernable
gladness of the soul.[2]    Then comes the secluded
colloquy between queen and princess,[3] as they discuss the guest who made the night so strange and
new; and then the rush of Dido's gathering passion
among the majestic symbols of her sway.[4]

"With him the queen the long ways wanders down,
  And shows him Sidon's wealth and Carthage town,
  And oft would speak, but as the words begin
Fails her breath caught by mastering Love within;—
  Once more in feast must she the night employ,
  Must hear once more her Trojan tell of Troy,
  Hang on his kingly voice, and shuddering see
The imagined scenes where every scene is he.
  Then guests are gone and night and morn are met,
  Far off in heaven the solemn stars have set,—
  Thro' the empty halls alone she mourns again,
Lies on the couch where hath her hero lain,
  Sees in the dark his kingly face, and hears
  His voice imagined in her amorous ears."

And through all the scenes that follow, the same
royal accent runs till the last words that lift our
imagination from the tumultuous grief around the
dying Dido, to the scarce more terrible tragedy of
a great nation's fall.[5]

[1] A. i. 725.          [2] A. i. 738.          [3] A. iv. 10
    [4] A. iv. 74.          [5] A. iv. 669.

" Not else than thus, when foes have forced a way,
  On Tyre or Carthage falls the fatal day ;—
  'Mid such wild woe crash down in roaring fire
  Temples and towers of Carthage or of Tyre."

And assuredly the " Deeds of the Roman People,"[1]
the title which many men gave to the Æneid when
it first appeared, would not have been complete
without some such chapter as this.   The prophecy
of Anchises, the shield of Vulcan, record for us the
imperial city's early virtue, her world-wide sway ;
but it is in this tale of Carthage that the poet has
written in a burning parable the passion and the
pomp of Rome.

And yet in spite of all the force and splendour
with which Dido is described, we feel instinctively
that she is not drawn by a lover's hand.   We have
in her no indication of the poet's own ideal and
inward dream.   If that is to be sought at all, it
must be sought elsewhere.   And, perhaps, if the
fancy be permitted, we may imagine that we discern
it best in the strange and yearning beauty of the
passages which speak of the glorious girlhood of
Camilla, the maid unwon ; Camilla, whose death a
nymph avenges, and whose tale Diana tells; Camilla,
whose name leapt first of all to Virgil's lips as he
spoke to Dante of their Italy in the underworld.[2]
Surely there is something more than a mere poetic fervour in the lines which describe the love which lit on

---

[1] " Gesta populi Romani."          [2] Inf. i. 107.

the girl while yet a child, and followed her till her
glorious hour;[1] the silent reverence which watched
the footsteps of the maiden " whom so many mothers
for their sons desired in vain ; "[2] the breath caught
with a wistful wonder, the long and lingering gaze,[3]
the thrill of admiration which stirs the heart with
the very concord of joy and pain.   Where has he
more subtly mingled majesty with sweetness than in
the lines which paint her happy nurture among the
woodlands where her father was a banished king?
her wild and supple strength enhanced by the contrasting thought of the "flowing gown and golden
circlet,"[4] which might have weighted the free limbs
with royal purple or wound among the tresses that
were hooded with the tiger's spoil.

Thus much, at least, we may say, that while in
poetry the higher and truer forms of love, as distin-
guished both from friendship and from passion,
appear first in the Middle Ages, and in Dante above
all, yet passages like these reveal to us the early stirring of conceptions which were hereafter to be so
dominant and so sublime—the dawning instinct of

---

[1] A. xi. 537.                    [2] A. xi. 581.

[3] Illam omnis tectis agrisque effusa inventus
   Turbaque miratur matrum et prospectat euntem,
   Attonitis inhians animis, ut regius ostro
   Velet honos levis humeros, ut fibula crinem.
   Auro internectat, Lyciam ut gerat ipsa pharetram
   Et pastoralem praefixa cuspide myrtum.—A. vii. 812.

[4] Pro crinali auro, pro longae tegmine pallae
   Tigridis exuviae per dorsum a vertice pendent, etc.- A. xi. 576.

a worship which should be purer and more pervading than any personal desire—of a reverence which should have power for a season to keep Love himself at bay, and to which a girl's gladness and beauty should become a part " of something far more deeply interfused," and touch the spirit with the same sense of yearning glory which descends on us from the heaven of stars.

To dwell thus on some of the passages in Virgil whose full meaning escapes a hasty perusal, may help us to realise one of his characteristic charms —his power of concentrating the strangeness and fervour of the romantic spirit within the severe and dignified limits of classical art. To this power in great measure we must ascribe his unique position as the only unbroken link between the ancient and the modern world. In literary style and treatment, just as in religious dogma and tendency, there has been something in him which has appealed in turn to ages the most discrepant and the most remote. He has been cited in different centuries as an authority on the worship of river-nymphs and on the incarnation of Christ. And similarly the poems which were accepted as soon as published as the standard of Latin classicality, became afterwards the direct or indirect original of half the Renaissance epics of adventure and love.

We feel, however, that considerations like these leave us still far from any actual realisation of the

means by which the poet managed to produce this
singular complex of impressions.   In dealing with
poetry, as with the kindred arts, criticism almost
necessarily ceases to be fruitful or definite at the
very point where the interest of the problems becomes the greatest. * We must be content with such
narrower inquiries as may give us at least a clearer
conception of the nature and difficulties of the
achievement at which the artist has aimed.   We
may, for instance, discuss the capabilities of the
particular language in which a poet writes, just as
we may discuss the kind of effects producible on
violin or pianoforte, in water-colour or oil.   And
any estimate of the Latin, as a literary language,
implies at once a comparison with the speech of
that people from whose admirable productions Latin
literature was avowedly derived.

No words that men can any more set side by
side can ever affect the mind again like some of the
great passages of Homer.   For in them it seems as
if all that makes life precious were in the act of
being created at once and together—language itself,
and the first emotions, and the inconceivable charm
of song.   When we hear one single sentence of
Anticleia's answer,[1] as she begins—

οὔτ᾽ ἐμέγ᾽ ἐν μεγάροισιν ἐύσκοπος ἰοχέαιρα—

what words can express the sense which we receive

---

[1] Od. xi. 198.

of an effortless and absolute sublimity, the feeling
of morning freshness and elemental power, the
delight which is to all other intellectual delights
what youth is to all other joys? And what a
language! which has written, as it were, of itself
those last two words for the poet, which offers them
as the fruit of its inmost structure and the bloom
of its early day! Beside speech like this Virgil's
seems elaborate, and Dante's crabbed, and Shakespeare's barbarous. There never has been, there
never will be, a language like the dead Greek. For
Greek had all the merits of other tongues without
their accompanying defects. It had the monu-
mental weight and brevity of the Latin without its
rigid unmanageability; the copiousness and flexi-
bility of the German without its heavy commonness
and guttural superfluity; the pellucidity of the
French without its jejuneness; the force and reality
of the English without its structureless comminu-
tion. But it was an instrument beyond the control
of any but its creators. When the great days of
Greece were past, it was the language which made
speeches and wrote books, and not the men. Its
French brilliancy taught Isocrates to polish platitude
into epigram; its German profundity enabled Lyco-
phron to pass off nonsense as oracles; its Italian
flow encouraged Apollonius Rhodius to shroud in
long-drawn sweetness the langour of his inventive
soul. There was nothing except the language left.

Like the golden brocade in a queen's sepulchre, its imperishable splendour was stretched stiffly across the skeleton of a life and thought which inhabited there no more.

The history of the Latin tongue was widely different. We do not meet it full-grown at the dawn of history; we see it take shape and strength beneath our eyes. We can watch, as it were, each stage in the forging of the thunderbolt; from the day when Ennius, Nævius, Pacuvius inweave their "three shafts of twisted storm,"[1] till Lucretius adds "the sound and terror," and Catullus "the west wind and the fire." It grows with the growth of the Roman people; it wins its words at the sword's point; and the "conquered nations in long array" pay tribute of their thought and speech as surely as of their blood and gold.

In the region of poetry this union of strenuous effort with eager receptivity is conspicuously seen. The barbarous Saturnian lines, hovering between an accentual and a quantitative system, which were the only indigenous poetical product of Latium, rudely indicated the natural tendency of the Latin tongue towards a trochaic rhythm. Contact with Greece introduced Greek metres, and gradually established a definite quantitative system. Quantity and accent are equally congenial to the Latin lan-

---

[1] Tris imbris torti radios, tris nubis aquosae
Addiderant, rutili tris ignis et alitis Austri.  A. viii. 429.

guage, and the trochaic and iambic metres of Greece
bore transplantation with little injury.　The adaptations of these rhythms by early Roman authors,
however uncouth, are at least quite easy and un-
constrained; and so soon as the prestige of the
Augustan era had passed away, we find both Pagans
and Christians expressing in accentual iambic, and
especially in accentual trochaic metres, the thoughts
and feelings of the new age.　Adam of S. Victor is
metrically nearer to Livius Andronicus than to
Virgil or Ovid; and the Litany of the Arval
Brethren finds its true succession, not in the Secular
Ode of Horace, but in the *Dies Iræ* or the *Veni
Creator.*

For Latin poetry suffered a violent breach of
continuity in the introduction from Greece ,of the
hexameter and the elegiac couplet.　The quantitative hexameter is in Latin a difficult and unnatural
metre.　Its prosodial structure excludes a very large
proportion of Latin words from being employed at
all.　It narrowly limits the possible grammatical
constructions, the modes of emphasis, the usages of
curtailment, the forms of narration.　On the other
hand, when successfully managed its advantages are
great.　All the strength and pregnancy of Latin
expression are brought .out by the stately march of
a metre perhaps the most compact and majestic
which has ever been invented.　The words take
their place like the organs in a living structure--—

close packed but delicately adjusted and mutually supporting. And the very sense of difficulty overcome gives an additional charm to the sonorous beauty of the dactylic movement, its self-retarding pauses, its onward and overwhelming flow.

To the Greek the most elaborate poetical effects were as easy as the simplest. In his poetic, as in his glyptic art, he found all materials ready to his hand; he had but to choose between the marble and the sardonyx, between the ivory and the gold. The Roman hewed his conceptions out of the granite rock; oftenest its craggy forms were rudely piled together, yet dignified and strong; but there were hands which could give it finish too, which could commit to the centuries a work splendid as well as imperishable, polished into the basalt's shimmer and fervent with the porphyry's glow.

It must not, however, be supposed that even the Æneid has wholly overcome the difficulties inseparable from the Latin poetry of the classical age, that it is entirely free either from the frigidities of an imitation or from the constraints of a *tour de force*. In the first place, Virgil has not escaped the injury which has been done to subsequent poets by the example of the length and the subject-matter of Homer. An artificial dignity has been attached to poems in twelve or twenty-four books, and authors have been incited to tell needlessly long stories in order to take rank as epic poets. And because

Homer is full of tales of personal combat—in his day an exciting and all-important thing — later poets have thought it necessary to introduce a large element of this kind of description, which, so soon as it loses reality, becomes not only frigid but disgusting.   It is as if the first novel had been written by a schoolboy of genius, and all succeeding novelists had felt bound to construct their plots mainly of matches at football.   It is the later books of the Æneid that are most marred by this mistake. In the earlier books there are, no doubt, some ill-judged adaptations of Homeric incident,[1] some laboured reproductions of Homeric formulæ, but for the most part the events are really noble and pathetic,—are such as possess permanent interest for civilised men.   The three last books, on the other hand, which have come down to us in a crude and unpruned condition, contain large tracts immediately imitated from Homer, and almost devoid of independent value.[2]

Besides these defects in matter, the latter part of the poem illustrates the metrical dangers to which Latin hexameters succumbed almost as soon as Virgil was gone.   The types on which they could be composed were limited in number and were becoming exhausted.   Many of the lines in

[1] See especially A. v. 263-5.

[2] The following passages might perhaps be omitted *en bloc* with little injury to Virgil's reputation :—A. x. 276-762 ; xi. 597-648, 868-908 ; xii. 266-311, 529-592.

the later books are modelled upon lines in the
earlier ones.   Many passages show that peculiar
form of bald artificiality into which this difficult
metre so readily sinks; nay, some of the *tibicines*,
or stop-gaps, suggest a grotesque resemblance to the
well-known style of the fourth-form boy.[1]   Other
more ambitious passages give the painful impression
of just missing the effect at which they aim.[2]

We should, however, be much mistaken if we
inferred that this accidental want of finish—due to
the poet's premature death—indicated any decline
of power.   On the contrary, nothing, perhaps, in
Latin versification is more interesting than the
traces of a later manner in process of formation,
which are to be found in the concluding books of
the Æneid.   The later manner of a painter or poet
generally differs from his earlier manner in much
the same way.   We observe in him a certain im-
patience of the rules which have guided him to
excellence, a certain desire to use materials more
freely, to obtain bolder and newer effects.   A
tendency of this kind may be discerned in the
versification of the later books, especially of the
twelfth book, of the Æneid.   The innovations are
individually hardly perceptible, but taken together
they alter the character of the hexameter line in a
way more easily felt than described.   Among the
more definite changes we may note that there are

[1] *e.g.* A. x. 526-9, 584-5.     [2] *e.g.* A. x. 468-471, 557-560.

more full stops in the middle of lines, there are
more elisions, there is a larger proportion of short
words, there are more words repeated, more asson-
ances, and a freer use of the emphasis gained by
the recurrence of verbs in the same or cognate
tenses. Where passages thus characterised have
come down to us still in the making, the effect
is forced and fragmentary.[1] Where they succeed
they combine, as it seems to me, in a novel manner
the rushing freedom of the old trochaics with the
majesty which is the distinguishing feature of
Virgil's style.[2] Art has concealed its art, and the
poet's last words suggest to us possibilities in the
Latin tongue which no successor has been able to
realise.

It is difficult to dwell long on such technical
points as these without appearing arbitrary or pe-
dantic. The important thing is to understand how
deliberate, forceful, weighty, Virgil's diction is; what
a mass of thought and feeling was needed to give to
the elaborate structure of the Latin hexameter any
convincing power; how markedly all those indications by which we instinctively judge the truth or
the insincerity of an author's emotion are intensified
by a form of composition in which " the style," not
only of every paragraph but of every clause, is

[1] *e.g.* A. x. 597-600.
[2] *e.g.* A. xii. 48, 72, 179, 429, 615-6, 632-649, 676-680, 889-893,
903-4.

necessarily and indeed " the man." And when we have learned by long familiarity to read between the lines, to apportion the emphasis, to reproduce, it may be, in imagination some shadow of that " marvellous witchery "[1] with which, as tradition tells us, Virgil's own reading of his poems brought out their beauty, we shall be surprised at the amount of self-revelation discernible beneath the calm of his impersonal song. And here again we shall receive the same impression which remained with us from the examination of the hero who is thought to be in some measure the unconscious portrait of the poet himself—we shall wonder most of all at the abiding sadness of his soul.

We might have thought to find him like the steersman Palinurus, in the scene from which our great English painter has taken the cadence which is to tell of an infinite repose,[2] communing untroubled with some heaven-descended dream, and keeping through the night's tranquillity his eyes still fixed upon the stars. How is it that he appears to us so often, like the same Palinurus, plunged in a solitary gulf of death, while the ship of human destinies drifts away unguided—*trostlos auf weitem Meer?* How knew he that gathering horror of midnight which presages some unspeakable ruin and the end of all?[3] Why was it left for him, above all men, to tell of the anguish of irredeemable bereavement, and Eurydice's

---

[1] " Lenociniis miris."

[2] Turner's Datur Hora Quieti. A. v. 844.   [3] A. iv. 460-4

appealing hands as she vanished backwards into the
night?[1] What taught him the passion of those lines
whose marvellous versification seems to beat with
the very pulses of the heart,[2] where the one soul calls
upon the other in the many-peopled fields of death,
and asks of all that company, "not less nor more, but
even that word alone"? What is it that has given
such a mystical intensity to every glimpse which he
opens of the eternity of the impassioned soul?—
where sometimes the wild pathetic rhythm alone
suggests an undefinable regret,[3] or a single epithet
will renew a world of mourning, and disclose a sorrow unassuageable in Paradise itself.[4] Or, for one
moment, Sychaeus' generous shade, appealed to in
such varying accents as the storms of passion rose
or fell, deemed sometimes forgetful and distant and
unregarding in the grave, is seen at last in very
presence and faithful to the vows of earth, filled
with a love which has forgiven inconstancy as it has
outlasted death.[5]

These short and pregnant passages will appeal to
different minds with very different power. There
are some whose emotion demands a fuller expression
than this, a more copious and ready flow—who choose
rather, like Shelley, to pour the whole free nature
into a sudden and untrammelled lay. But there are
others who have learnt to recognise the last height

---

[1] G. iv. 498.          [2] A. vi. 670.
[3] A. vi. 447.     [4] A. vi. 480.     [5] A. vi. 474.

of heroism, the last depth of tenderness, rather in a
word than in a protest, and rather in a look than in a
word; to whom all strong feeling comes as a purging
fire, a disengagement from the labyrinth of things;
whose passion takes a more concentrated dignity as
it turns inwards and to the deep of the heart. And
such men will recognise in Virgil a precursor, a master,
and a friend; they will call him the *Magnanimo*, the
*Verace Duca;* they will enrol themselves with eager
loyalty among the spiritual progeny of a spirit so
melancholy, august, and alone.

And some, too, there will always be to whom
some touch of poetic gift has revealed the delight of
self-expression, while yet their infertile instinct of
melody has failed them at their need, and their
scanty utterance has rather mocked than assuaged for
them the incommunicable passion of the soul. Such
men will be apt to think that not only would an
added sanctity have been given to all sacred sorrow,
an added glory to all unselfish joy, but that this
earth's less ennobling emotions as well—the sting
of unjust suspicions,[1] and the proud resentment of
stealthy injuries,[2] and the bewilderment of life's unguided way[3]—even these would have been trans-
muted into spiritual strength if they could in such
manner have shaped themselves into song; as the
noise of bear, and wolf, and angered lion came to the
Trojans with a majesty that had no touch of fear or

[1] A. i. 529.        [2] A. vi. 502.        [3] A. xii. 917.

pain, as they heard them across the midnight waters, mixed with the music of Circe's echoing isle.[1]

How was it, then, with the poet himself, to whom it was given to " sweep in ever-highering eagle-circles up" till his words became the very term and limit of human utterance in song ?  *Quin Decios Drusosque procul ;*—when he was summing up in those lines like bars of gold the hero-roll of the Eternal City, conferring with every word an immortality, and, like his own Æneas, bearing on his shoulders the fortune and the fame of Rome, did he feel in that great hour that he had done all that man can do ?  All that we know is, that he spoke of his attempt to write the Æneid as " an act almost of insanity," and that on his deathbed he urgently begged his friends to burn the unfinished poem.

> " O dignitosa coscienza e netta,
> Come t'è picciol fallo amaro morso ! "

Yet we feel that Virgil's character would not have stood out complete to us without the record of that last desire.  It was the culminating expression of a lifelong temper—of that yearning after perfection which can never rest satisfied with the things of earth—which carries always with it, as Plato would say, the haunting reminiscence of that perfect beauty on which the soul has looked aforetime in the true, which is the ideal world.  And the very stillness

---

[1] A. vii. 10.

and dignity of Virgil's outward existence help to make him to us an unmixed example of this mood of mind. There is no trace in him of egoistic passion, of tumult, of vanity, or of any jealous or eager love; all his emotions seem to have fused or melted into that *Welt-Schmerz*—that impersonal and indefinable melancholy, the sound of which since his day has grown so familiar in our ears, which invades the sanest and the strongest spirits, and seems to yield to nothing except such a love, or such a faith, as can give or promise heaven. The so-called "modern air" in Virgil's poems is in great measure the result of the constantly-felt pressure of this obscure home-sickness—this infinite desire; finding vent sometimes in such appeals as forestall the sighs of Christian saints in the passion of high hopes half withdrawn, when the Divinity is shrouded and afar[1]—oftener perceptible only in that accent of brooding sorrow which mourns over the fate of men, and breathes a pathetic murmur into Nature's peace,[2] and touches with a mysterious forlornness the felicity of the underworld.[3]

It is the same mood which "intenerisce il cuore" in Dante's song, which looks from the unsatisfied eyes of Michael Angelo and of Tintoret,—a mood commoner, indeed, among the nations of the North,

---

[1] *e.g.* G. iv. 324-5.  A. i. 407.

[2] Te nemus Anguitiae, vitrea te Fucinus unda,
Te liquidi flevere lacus.  A. vii. 760.

[3] Solemque suum, sua sidera nôrunt.  A. vi. 641.

but felt at times by Italians who have had the power to see that all the glory round them does but add a more mysterious awfulness to the insoluble riddle of the world.

Nor is any region of Italy a fitter temple for such thoughts than the Bay of Naples, which virtually was Virgil's home. For it was not Mantua, but "sweet Parthenope," which fostered his years of silent toil; his wanderings were on that southern shore where the intense and azure scene seems to carry an unknown sadness in the convergence of heaven and sea, and something of an unearthly expectancy in the still magnificence of its glow. It was there that inwardly he bled and was comforted, inwardly he suffered and was strong; it was there that what others learn in tempest he learnt in calm, and became in ardent solitude the very voice and heart of Rome.

## II.

The century which elapsed between the publication of the Fourth Eclogue and of the Epistle to the Romans witnessed an immense expansion of the human mind. So far as we can attach definite dates to the gradual growth of world-wide conceptions, we may say that in this century arose the ideas of the civil and of the religious unity of all families of men. These ideas, at first apparently hostile to one another, and associated, the one with the military supremacy

of Rome, the other with the spiritual supremacy of
Jerusalem, gradually coalesced into the notion of a
Holy Roman Empire, involving, as that notion does
in the mind, for instance, of Dante, the concentration
of both spiritual and temporal power in the Eternal
City.   Again the conceptions have widened; and we
now imagine a brotherhood of mankind, a universal
Church, without localised empire or a visible vice-
gerent of heaven.

Throughout all the phases which these great
generalisations have traversed, the authority of Virgil
has been freely invoked.   And when we turn from
the personal to the public aspect of his poems, we
are at once obliged to discuss in what sense he may
be considered as the earliest and the official exponent
of the world-wide Empire of Rome, the last and the
closest precursor of the world-wide commonwealth of
Christ.   The unanimous acceptance of Virgil in his
lifetime—while the Æneid was yet unwritten—as
the unique poetical representative of the Roman
State is a fact quite as surprising and significant as
the ready acceptance of Augustus as its single ruler.
It is not, indeed, strange that a few short but lovely
pieces, such as the Eclogues, should have delighted
literary circles and suggested to Mæcenas that this
young poet's voice would be the fittest to preach the
revival of antique simplicity and rural toil.   The
astonishing thing is the success of the Georgics, the
fact that an agricultural poem not twice as long as

*Comus* should at once have procured for its author a
reputation to which the literary history of the world
affords no parallel. Petrarch was crowned on the
Capitol amid the applause of the literati of Europe.
Voltaire was "smothered with roses" in the crowded
theatres of the Paris of his old age. But the triumph
of Petrarch was the manifesto of a humanistic clique.
The triumph of Voltaire was the first thunderclap
of a political storm. When, on the other hand, the
Romans rose to their feet in the theatre on the casual
quotation of some words of Virgil's on the stage—
when they saluted the poet as he entered the house
with the same marks of reverence which they paid
to Augustus Cæsar—it was plain that some cause
was at work which was not of a partisan, which was
not even of a purely literary character. Perhaps it
was that the minds of men were agitated by the
belief that a new era was impending, that "the great
order of the ages was being born anew," and in the
majestic and catholic tranquillity of Virgil's song they
recognised instinctively the temper of an epoch no
longer of struggle but of supremacy, the first-fruits
of Imperial Rome. We must at least attribute some
such view to the cultivated classes of the time. That
the sublime poem of Lucretius should obtain only
a cold *succès d'estime*, while the Georgics, a more exquisite work, no doubt, but a work of so much smaller
range, should be hailed as raising its author to an
equality with Homer, is a disproportion too great to

be accounted for by a mere literary preference. It was a deep-seated recognition of the truly national character of Virgil's work, of his unique fitness to reflect completely all the greatness of the advancing time, which led even rival poets to predict so strenuously that the Æneid, of which no one had as yet seen a paragraph, would be co-eternal with the dominion of Rome. Stranger still it is to see how tragically the event surpassed the prophecy. "Light among the vanished ages," we may exclaim with no exaggeration, in Lord Tennyson's words—

> "Star that gildest yet this phantom shore!
> Golden branch amid the shadows, kings and realms that
>     set to rise no more!"

When we look at the intellectual state of Rome in the fourth and fifth centuries, our complaint is not that Virgil is forgotten, but that nothing else is remembered; that the last achievement of the "toga-wearing race" is to extemporise centos from the Æneid on any given theme; that the last heads seen to rise above the flood of advancing barbarism should be those of grammarians calling themselves Menalcas and parsing *Tityre*, or calling themselves Virgilius and parsing *Arma virum*.

There is something, too, of Fate's solemn irony in the way in which, as the ancient world is re-discovered, the first words borne back to us by the muffled voice of ruin or catacomb are scattered

fragments of that poem which was the last on
Rome's living lips.   There is something tragic in
finding Virgil's line, "So great a work it was to
found the race of Rome," cut in colossal characters
on the monstrous ruins of the baths of Titus;
Virgil's words, "Then all were silent," look strangely
in a half-finished scrawl .from a wall of Pompeii's
hushed and solitary homes.[1]    But the long tradition,
as has been already said, has not continued unbroken to our own day.   There have of late been
many critics who have denied that the Æneid is
adequately representative of the Roman commonwealth, who have been struck with the unqualified
support, the absolute deification bestowed on
Augustus, and have urged that the laureate who
indulged in so gratuitous an adulation must be
styled a court, and not a national poet.

So far as Virgil's mere support of Augustus
goes, this objection, however natural to the lovers
of free government, will hardly stand the test of
historical inquiry.   For Virgil had not to choose
between Augustus and the Republic, but between
Augustus and Antony.   The Republic was gone for
ever; and not Hannibal himself, we may surely
say, was a more dangerous foe than Antony to the
Roman people.   No battle which that people ever
fought was more thoroughly national, more decis-
ively important, than the battle of Actium.   The

[1] CONTICVEREOM.

name of Actium, indeed, can never waken the glory
and the joy which spring to the heart at the name
of Salamis.    Not "Leucate's promontory afire with
embattled armaments," not " Actian Apollo bending
from above his bow " can stir the soul like that one
trump,[1] that morning onset, that "small ill-har-
boured islet, oft-haunted of dance-loving Pan." [2]
But the essence of each battle was in fact the same.
Whether it were against the hosts of Susa and
Ecbatana, or against "the dog Anubis" and the
Egyptian queen, each battle was the triumph of
Western discipline, religion, virtue, over the tide of
sensuality and superstition which swept onwards
from the unfathomable East.

And thus we come to the point where Virgil
is, in reality, closely identified with the policy of
the Augustan *régime.*    Augustus was not himself
a moral hero.    But partly fortune, partly wisdom,
partly a certain innate preference for order and
reverence for the gods, had rendered him the only
available representative, not only of the constitution
and the history, but of the morals and religion of
Rome.    The leading pre-occupation of his official
life was the restoration of national virtue.    It is
hard to trace the success or failure of an attempt
like this among a complex society's conflicting
currents of good and evil.    Yet it seems that to his
strenuous insistance on all of morality which

[1] Aesch. Pers. 395.          [2] Psyttalea. Pers. 447.

legislation can achieve, we may in some measure ascribe that moonlight of Roman virtue which mingles so long its chastened gentleness with the blaze of the Empire's lurid splendour, the smoke of its foul decay.　A reform like this, however, cannot be achieved by a single ruler.　And sincere co-operation was hard to find.　Papius and Poppæus might pass laws against celibacy.　But Papius and Poppæus themselves (as Boissier reminds us) remained obstinately unmarried.　Horace might sing of praying to the gods "with our wives and children."　But no one was ever less than Horace of a church-goer or a family man.　Virgil, on the other hand, was one of those men whose adherence seems to give reality to any project of ethical reform.　The candid and serious poet, "than whom," as Horace says, "earth bore no whiter soul," was quickly recognised by Mæcenas as the one writer who could with sincerity sound the praises of antique and ingenuous virtue.　The Georgics came to the Roman world somewhat as the writings of Rousseau came to the French; they might have little apparent influence upon conduct, but they made a new element in the mind of the age, they testified at least to the continued life of pure ideas, to the undying conception of a contented labour, of an unbought and guileless joy.

But this was not yet enough.　The spirit of Roman virtue needed to be evoked by a sterner spell.　In

the Georgics the land of Italy had for the first time
been impressively presented as a living and organic
whole.   And the idea of Italy's lovely primacy
among all other countries was destined to subsist
and grow.   But it was not yet towards the name of
Italy that the enthusiasm of Virgil's fellow-citizens
most readily went out.   However variously expressed
or shrouded, the religion of the Romans was Rome.
The destiny of the Eternal City is without doubt
the conception which, throughout the long roll of
human history, has come nearest to the unchange-
able and the divine.   It is an idea majestic enough
to inspire worship, and to be the guide of life and
death.   This religion of Rome, in its strictest sense,
has formed no trifling factor in the story of the
Christian Church.   It appears in its strongest and
most unquestioning form in the De Monarchia of
Dante.   It formed a vital part of the creed of the
great Italian who in our own century has risen to
closest communion in thought and deed with the
heroes of his country's past.   But nowhere, from
Ennius to Mazzini, has this faith found such expression as in Virgil's Æneid.   All is there.   There
is nothing lacking of noble reminiscence, of high
exhortation, of inspiring prophecy.   Roman virtue
is appealed to through the channel by which alone
it could be reached and could be restored; it is
renewed by majestic memories and stimulated by
an endless hope.   The Georgics had been the psalm

of Italy, the Æneid was the sacred book of the
Religion of Rome.

It appears, then, that although Virgil doubtless
lent all his weight to the personal government of
Augustus, he neither chose that government in preference to any attainable form of stable freedom,
nor co-operated with it in an unfitting manner, nor
with an unworthy aim.   There remains the question
of the deification of Augustus — of the impulse
given by Virgil to that worship of the emperors
which ultimately became so degrading and so cruel
a farce.   And here, no doubt, in one passage at
least, Virgil's language is such as modern taste must
condemn.   The frigid mythology with which the
first Georgic opens is absolutely bad.   It is bad as
Callimachus is bad, and as every other imitation of
Callimachus in Latin literature is bad too.   It has,
indeed, little meaning; and what meaning it has
would need an astrologer to decipher.   What are
we to make of Tethys and of Proserpine, of Thule
and of Elysium, or of the Scorpion who is willing
to draw in his claws to make room for Augustus in
heaven ?   It has, indeed, been ingeniously suggested
that the true point of this strange passage may con-
sist in a veiled but emphatic warning to Augustus
not to assume the title of King,[1] (a title of which,
as in Caligula's case, the Romans were far more
chary than of the less practical ascription of god-

[1] G. i. 36-7. The suggestion is Mr. Raper's.

head); and, moreover, that the poet himself sub-sequently apologises[1] for the unreality of the flattering exordium in which this lesson is concealed. Still, we must regret that any passage in Virgil should require such apology. We cannot help seeing more dignity in the tone of Lucretius, whose only feeling with regard to earthly potentates was vexation at their being too busy to allow him to explain his philosophy to them as fully as he could have wished.[2]

The passages in the Æneid in which Augustus is prospectively deified stand on a different footing. In them he is more or less closely identified with Rome herself; he is represented as we see him in the great allegorical statue of the Vatican, — "Augustus Cæsar leading the Italians on to war, with the Senate and the people and the tutelary gods of Rome,"[3] the creation of that early moment in the empire's history when it seemed as if the conflicting currents of the Commonwealth might run at length in a single channel, and the State be symbolised not unworthily in the man whom she had chosen as her chief. And, indeed, when we consider the proportions which the worship of "Rome and the genius of Augustus" gradually assumed, the earnestness with which it was pressed on by the people in face of what seems to have been the genuine disapproval of the cautious Emperor,

---

[1] G. ii. 45-6.　　[2] Lucr. i. 43.　　[3] A. viii. 678.

the speed with which it became, without formal
change or definite installation, the practical religion
of the Roman world,[1] we shall see reason to suppose
that this strange form of worship, to which Virgil
gave perhaps the earliest, though in part an unconscious expression, was not the birth of a merely
meaningless servility, but represented what was in
fact a religious reform and a return to the oldest
instincts of the Roman people.

The Roman religion, as we first hear of it, shows
us an Aryan tradition already strongly modified by
the Roman character, by a tone of mind abstract
and juristic, rather than creative or joyous. Some
of the natural powers whose worship the earliest
Romans, in common with the earliest Greeks, had
inherited from their Aryan ancestors had already
acquired a definite quasi-human personality. These
the Roman necessarily accepted as persons, though
he added no fresh vividness to the conception of
them. But his feeble instinct of anthropomorphism
hardly went farther than this; and such deities as
he himself created,—such tutelary powers, I should
rather say, as he thought might be useful if they

[1] See M. Boissier's *Religion Romaine* on all this subject, and
especially for an account of the colleges of Augustales, which were
the earliest trade-guilds, the earliest representative bodies, the
model followed in Christian ecclesiastical organisation, and the
first religious bodies on a large scale which admitted all men, without distinction of wealth or birth, to a full share in their privileges
and in their control.

happened to exist,——were individualised in the most
shadowy manner.    They were little more than the
sublimated counterparts or correspondences of acts
or beings visible here on earth.    These deified
abstractions were of very various magnitude and
dignity, ranging from Minerva, Goddess of Memory,
and Janus, God of Opening, down to the crowd of
divinities little heard of outside the *Indigitamenta*
or handy-book of the Gods, the Goddess of Going
Out and the Goddess of Coming In, the God of
Silver Money and his father the God of Copper
Money, and the God of Speaking Intelligibly, who
never made more than a single remark.[1]    As the
Romans came into contact with other nations,
especially with Greece, foreign deities were introduced; but these were identified as far as possible
with the Roman deities of similar functions, and did
not overthrow the balance of the old *régime*.    But
as the strange Eastern gods, with their gloomy or
frenzied worships, were added to the list this quiet
absorption was no longer possible.    The Roman
Olympus came to resemble a shifting and turbulent
Convention, in which now one and now another
member,——Dionysus, Isis, Cybele,——rises tumultu-
ously into predominance, and is in turn eclipsed by
some newer arrival.    This inroad of furious and
conflicting superstitions had begun in Virgil's time,
and the battle of Actium is for him the defeat of

[1] Iterduca, Domiduca, Argentinus, Æsculanus, Aius Locutius.

the "monstrous forms of gods of every birth,"[1] who would have made their entry with Antony into Rome. At the same time it was hard to suggest an effective antidote for these degrading worships. The gods, so to speak, of the middle period—Jupiter and Juno and the like, with a Greek personality super-added to their more abstract significance—had not vitality enough to expel the intruders from their domain. It was necessary to fall back upon a more thoroughly national and primitive conception, and to deify once more the abstraction of the one earthly existence whose greatness was overwhelmingly evident—the power of Rome. The "Fortune of the City," or *Roma* herself enthroned with the insignia of a Goddess, was the only queen who could overrule at once the epidemic fanaticisms of Rome and the localised cults of the provinces, and be the veritable mistress of heaven.

Nor was even she enough. Through the abstractions of the old Roman religion there had always run a thread of more intimate and personal worship. Not only had each action and each object its spiritual counterpart, but each man as well. The nature of these Lares was somewhat vaguely and obscurely conceived, but the dominant idea seems to have been that they acted as the tutelary genii of men during life, and after death became identical with their immortal part. The Roman worship of an-

---

[1] A. viii. 698.

cestors was indeed of a different kind from the hero-
worship of the Greeks.   It dwelt less on the idea
of superhuman help than on the idea of family
continuity.   The Romans had not the faith which
bade the Locrians leave a place always open in their
battle-ranks for the Oïlean Ajax to fill unseen ; but
they testified by daily offering and daily prayer to
their conviction of an immanent and familiar presence which turned the home itself into a never-
vacant shrine.   They asked no oracle from " Amphiaraus beneath the earth ; " but the images of his
curule ancestors gathered round about the dead
Fabius in the market-place, and welcomed him in
silence as he joined the majority of his kin.   It is
this spirit of piety which the plot of the Æneid is
designed to illustrate and to foster.   Æneas has
no wish to conquer Latium.   He enters it merely
because he is divinely instructed that it is in Italy,
the original home of his race, that he must continue
the worship of his own  progenitor Assaracus and of
the tutelary gods of Troy.   This point achieved he
asks for nothing more.   He introduces the worship
of Assaracus; but, it must be added, Assaracus is
never heard of again.   So remote and legendary a
personage could not become the binding link of the
Roman people.   Nor had the Roman commonwealth
ever yet stood in such a relation to any single family
as to permit the identification of their private Lares
with the Lares Præstites of the city of Rome.   But

the case was altered now. One family had risen to
an isolated pre-eminence which no Roman had
attained before. And by a singular chance this
same family combined a legendary with an actual
primacy. Augustus was at once the representative
of Assaracus and the master of the Roman world.
The Lares of Augustus were at once identical in a
certain sense with Augustus himself, and with the
public Penates worshipped immemorially in their
chapel in the heart of the city. And if, as is no
doubt the case, the worship of Roma and the Lares
augusti could claim in Virgil its half-unconscious
prophet, we may reply that this worship, however
afterwards debased, was in its origin and essence
neither novel nor servile, but national and antique;
and that until the rise of Christianity, towards which
Virgil stands in a yet more singular anticipatory
relation, it would have been hard to say what other
form of religion could at once have satisfied the
ancient instincts and bound together the remote
extremities of the Roman world.

The relation of Virgil to Christianity, to which
we now come, is an unexpectedly complex matter.
To understand it clearly, we must attempt to disentangle some of the threads of religious emotion
and belief which intertwine in varying proportions
throughout his successive poems.

"Reared among the woods and thickets," an
Italian country child, the counterpart of Words-

worth in the union of spiritual aspiration with rustic
simplicity in which his early years were spent,
Virgil, like Wordsworth, seemed singled out as the
poet and priest of nature.    And directly imitated
as his Eclogues are from Theocritus, a closer investi-
gation reveals the essential differences between the
nature of the two poets.    The idylls of Theocritus
are glowing descriptions of pastoral life, written by
a man who lives and enjoys that life, and cares for
no other ideal.    The Eclogues of Virgil have less of
consistency, but they have more of purpose.    They
are an advocacy, none the less impassioned because
indirect, of the charm of scenery and simple pleasures
addressed to a society leading a life as remote from
nature as the life of the French court in the days of
Rousseau.    Theocritus, delighting in everything connected with rural life, loves to paint with vigour
even its least dignified scenes.    Virgil—whom the
Neapolitans called the Maid, and who shrank aside
when any one looked at him—is grotesquely artificial
when he attempts to render the coarse *badinage* of
country clowns.    On the other hand, where the
emotion in Theocritus is pure and worthy, Virgil is
found at his side, with so delicate a reproduction of
his effects, that it is sometimes hard to say whether
the Greek or the Latin passage seems the more
spontaneous and exquisite.[1]    And there is a whole
region of higher emotions in which the Latin poet is

[1] Compare E. viii. 37, with Theocr. xi. 25.

alone. All Virgil's own are those sudden touches
of exalted friendship,[1] of exquisite tenderness,[2] of the
sadness and the mystery of love,[3] which seem to
murmur amid the bright flow of his pastoral poetry
of the deep source from whence it springs, as his
own Eridanus had his fountain in Paradise and the
underworld.[4] All Virgil's own, too, is the comprehending vision, the inward eye which looks back
through all man's wars and tumult to the new-
created mountains[5] and the primal spring,[6] and that
"wise passiveness" to which nature loves to offer
her consolation, which fills so often the interspace
between faiths decayed and faiths re-risen with a

---

[1] *e.g.* E. vi. 64. The whole of the tenth eclogue is an exquisite
example of the half-tender, half-sportive sympathy by which one
friend can best strengthen another in the heart's lesser troubles,
and the blank when light loves have flown. The delicate humour
of this eclogue has perplexed the German commentators, who
suggest (1) either that Virgil meant it as a parody on the fifth
eclogue, or (2) that Gallus was in fact dead when it was written,
and that the poem,—ostensibly composed to console him for being
jilted by an actress,—was, in reality, intended as a sort of funeral
psalm. I may notice here the improbability of the story that
Virgil altered the end of the Fourth Georgic, omitting a panegyric
on Gallus after Gallus' disgrace and death. The Georgics were
published B.C. 29, and Gallus died B.C. 26. It is hard to believe
that a long passage, constituting the conclusion and crown of the
most popular and best known poem that had ever appeared in
Rome, and deriving added interest from the political scandal involved, should, after being three years before the public, have
perished so utterly that not a line, not a fragment of a line, not an
allusion to the passage, should anywhere remain.

[2] *e.g.* E. iv. 60.　　[3] *e.g.* E. viii. 47.　　[4] A. vi. 658.

[5] E. vi. 40.　　　　　　　[6] G. ii. 338.

tranquillised abeyance of doubt and fear. "Pan
and old Silvanus and the sister nymphs;" Silenus
keeping the shepherds spell-bound till twilight with
his cosmic song; Proteus uttering his unwilling
oracles upon the solitary shore; Clymene singing of
love in the caverned water-world amid the rivers'
roaring flow;—what are all these but aspects and
images of that great mother who has for all her
children a message which sometimes seems only
the sweeter because its meaning can be so dimly
known?

Peculiar to Virgil, too, is that tone of expecta-
tion which recurs again and again to the hope of
some approaching union of mankind beneath a juster
heaven, which bids the shepherd look no longer on
the old stars with worn-out promises, but on a star
new-risen and more benign; which tells in that
mystical poem to which scholars know no key, how
the pure and stainless shepherd dies and is raised
to heaven, and begins from thence a gentle sway
which forbids alike the wild beast's ravin and the
hunter's cruel guile.[1]

"O great good news thro' all the woods that ran!
O psalm and praise of shepherds and of Pan!
The hills unshorn to heaven their voices fling;
Desert and wilderness rejoice and sing;
'A god he is! a god we guessed him then!
Peace on the earth he sends and joy to men.'"

[1] E. v. 58.

But it is, of course, the Fourth, or Messianic
Eclogue (known to the English reader in Pope's
paraphrase, *Ye nymphs of Solyma, begin the song*),
which has formed the principal point of union
between Virgil and the new faith.   In every age of
Christianity, from Augustine to Abelard, from the
Christmas sermon of Pope Innocent III. to the
Prælectiones Academicæ of the late Mr. Keble,
divines and fathers of the Church have asserted the
inspiration, and claimed the prophecies of this marvellous poem.   It was on the strength of this poem
that Virgil's likeness was set among the carven seers
in the Cathedral of Zamora.   It was on the strength
of this poem that in the Cathedrals of Limoges and
Rheims the Christmas appeal was made : " O Maro,
prophet of the Gentiles, bear thou thy witness unto
Christ ; " and the stately semblance of the Roman
gave answer in the words which tell how " the new
progeny has descended from heaven on high."   The
prophecy can claim œcumenical acceptance, regenera-
tive efficacy.   The poet Statius, the martyr Secun-
dianus, were said to have been made Christians
by its perusal.   And at the supreme moment of the
transference and reconstruction of the civil and
spiritual authority of the earth, the Emperor Constantine in his oration, "inscribed to the Assembly
of Saints and dedicated to the Church of God,"
commented on this poem in a Greek version, as
forming a link between the old and the new faiths,

as explaining the change of form, and justifying the historical continuity, of the religion of the civilised world.

And there is nothing in this which need either surprise or shock us.[1]   For, in reality, the link between Virgil and Christianity depended not on a

---

[1] There is, no doubt, a startling antithesis between the real and the supposed object of Virgil's prophecy.   For there can surely be little doubt (as Bishop Louth, Boissier, etc., have argued) that the Fourth Eclogue was written in anticipation of the birth of the child of Augustus (then Octavianus) and Scribonia—the notorious Julia, born B.C. 39, shortly after the peace of Brundusium.   The words "te consule" applied to Pollio make it most unlikely that he was the child's *father*.   On the other hand, it would have been quite in keeping with Virgil's stately courtesy to address to Pollio, Antony's representative and Virgil's friend, a congratulatory poem on the birth in his consulship of a child to Augustus, with whom Antony had just been reconciled.   Virgil was from the first one of the most ardent supporters of Augustus, and though the young heir of Cæsar was not as yet clearly the first man in Rome, still, the prestige of the Julian family alone could make the expressions of the poem seem other than extravagant.   Virgil no doubt desired to associate Pollio as closely as possible with the hopes of the Roman commonwealth.   But to speak of "a world at peace through Pollio's virtue" would have been no less than absurd. Moreover, the phrase, "thy Apollo is in the ascendant now," points clearly to Augustus, whose patron Apollo was.   The reason why the riddle was not explained is obvious.   The expected child turned out to be a girl—and a girl who perhaps gave rise to more scandal than any other member of her sex.   It is singular that the embarrassing failure of the prediction at the time has been the source of its extraordinary reputation afterwards, when the horoscope composed for Julia was fulfilled in Jesus Christ.   Like the arrow of Acestes (A. v. 520), the prophecy seemed to consume away in the clouds and burn itself into empty air—

> "Till days far off its mighty meaning knew,
> And seers long after sang the presage true."

misapplied prediction but on a moral sequence, a spiritual conformity. There was a time when both the apologists and the adversaries of Christianity were disposed to ignore its connection with preceding faiths. Exaggerated pictures of its miraculous diffusion were met by the sneers of Gibbon at the contagious spread of superstitions among the ruins of a wiser world. The tone of both parties has altered as historical criticism has advanced. It is recognised that it is only "in the fulness of time" that a great religious change can come; that men's minds must be prepared for new convictions by a need which has been deeply felt, and a habit of thought which has been slowly acquired. And in Virgil's time, as has already been said, the old dogmas were tending to disappear. But while in the lower minds they were corrupting into superstition, in the higher they were evaporating into a clearer air. The spiritual element was beginning to assert itself over the ceremonial. Instincts of catholic charity were beginning to put to shame the tribal narrowness of the older faith. Philosophy was issuing from the lecture-room into the forum and the street.

And thus it is that Virgil's poems lie at the watershed of religions. Filled as they are with Roman rites and Roman tradition, they contain also another element, gentler, holier, till then almost unknown; a change has passed over them like the

change which passes over a Norwegian midnight
when the rose of evening becomes silently the rose
of dawn.

It is strange to trace the alternate attraction and
repulsion which the early Christians felt towards
Virgil. Sometimes they allegorised the Æneid into
a kind of Siege of Man-soul, in which the fall, the
temptations, the deliverance of man, are recorded in
a figure. Sometimes they compiled Christianised
centos from his poems,—works which obtained such
authority that Pope Gelasius found it necessary to
pronounce *ex cathedrâ* that they formed no part of
the canon of Scripture. Sometimes, as in Augustine,
we watch the conflict in a higher air; we see the
ascetic absorption in the new faith at war with the
truer instinct, which warns him that all noble
emotions are in reality mutually supporting, and
that we debase instead of ennobling our devotion
to one supreme ideal if we shrink from recognising
the goodness and greatness of ideals which are not
to us so dear. But even in the wild legends which
in the Middle Ages cluster so thickly round the
name of Virgil, even in the distorted fancies of the
hamlet or the cloister, we can discern some glimmer-
ing perception of an actual truth. It is not true,
as the Spanish legend tells us, that " Virgil's eyes
first saw the star of Bethlehem ;" but it is true that
in none more fully than in him is found that temper
which offers all worldly wealth, all human learning,

at the feet of Purity, and for the knowledge of
Truth.   It is not true that Virgil was a magician;
that he clove the rock; that he wrought a gigantic
figure which struck a note of warning at the far-
seen onset of tumult or of war; but it is true that
he was one of those who "*like giants stand, to
sentinel enchanted land,*" whose high thoughts have
caught and reflect the radiance of some mysterious
and unrisen day.

Although the interest which subsequent ages
have taken in the religion of Virgil has turned
mainly upon his relation to Christianity, he would
himself, of course, have judged in another light the
growth of his inward being.   A celebrated passage
in the Georgics has revealed to us his mood of mind
in a decisive hour.   To understand it we must refer
to the strongest influence which his youth was
destined to undergo.   When Virgil was on the
threshold of life a poem was published which,
perhaps, of all single monuments of Roman genius,
conveys to us the most penetrating conception of
the irresistible force of Rome.   There is no need to
deck Lucretius with any attributes not his own.
We may grant that his poetry is often uncouth, his
science confused, his conception of human existence
steeped in a lurid gloom.   But no voice like his has
ever proclaimed the nothingness of "momentary
man," no prophet so convincing has ever thundered
in our ears the appalling Gospel of Death.   Few

minds, perhaps, that were not stiffly cased in fore-
gone conclusions have ever met the storm of his
passionate eloquence without bending before the
blast, without doubting for an hour of their inmost
instincts, and half believing that " as we felt no woe
in times long gone, when from all the earth to battle
the Carthaginians came," so now it may be man's
best and only hope to quench in annihilation his
unsated longings and his deep despair.

On Virgil's nature, disposed at once to vague
sadness and to profound inquiry, the six books on
the Nature of Things produced their maximum
effect. Alike in his thought and language we see
the Lucretian influence mingling with that spirit of
natural religion which seems to have been his own
earliest bent ; and at last, in the passage above referred to,[1] he pauses between the two hypotheses,
each alike incapable of proof ; that which assumes
that because we see in nature an impersonal order,
therefore there is no more to see, and that which
assumes that because we feel within us a living
spirit, the universe, too, lives around us and breathes
with the divine.

" If thou thy secrets grudge me, nor assign
    So high a lore to such a heart as mine,—
  Still, Nature, let me still thy beauty know,
  Love the clear streams that thro' thy valleys flow,

---

[1] G. ii. 490. The last two lines of the version here given
merely summarise a passage too long for quotation.

To many a forest lawn that love proclaim,
Breathe the full soul, and make an end of fame !
Ah me, Spercheos ! oh to watch alway
On Taygeta the Spartan girls at play !
Or cool in Hæmus' gloom to feel me laid,
Deep in his branching solitudes of shade !
   Happy the man whose steadfast eye surveys
The whole world's truth, its hidden works and ways, —
Happy, who thus beneath his feet has thrown
All fears and fates, and Hell's insatiate moan !—
Blest, too, were he the sister nymphs who knew,
Pan, and Sylvanus, and the sylvan crew ;—
On kings and crowds his careless glance he flings,
And scorns the treacheries of crowds and kings ;
Far north the leaguered hordes are hovering dim ;
Danube and Dacian have no dread for him ;
No shock of laws can fright his steadfast home,
Nor realms in ruin nor all the fates of Rome.
Round him no glare of envied wealth is shed,
From him no piteous beggar prays for bread ;
Earth, Earth herself the unstinted gift will give,
Her trustful children need but reap and live ;
She hath man's peace 'mid all the worldly stir,
One with himself he is, if one with her."

And henceforth without fanatical blindness, but
with a slow deliberate fervour, he elects to act upon
the latter opinion ; and from this time we find little
trace of the influence of Lucretius in his poems,
except it may be some quickening of that delight
in the hidden things of nature which makes the
world's creation Iopas',[1] as it was Silenus'[2] song ;

_____
[1] A. i. 743.                        [2] E. vi. 31

some deepening of that mournful wonder with which he regards the contrast between the hopes and fates of men.

And is there, then, anything in Virgil's creed more definite than this vague spirituality ? Is there any moral government of the world of which he can speak to us from the heart ? If so, it is not in connection with the old gods of Rome, for they have lost their individual life. They are no longer like those gods of Homer's, who "sat on the brow of Callicolone," awful in their mingling of aloofness and reality, of terror and subduing charm. Jove's frowns, Cytherea's caresses, in the Æneid assume alike an air of frigid routine. And in the unfinished later books the references to the heavenly council-board are of so curt and formal a character that they can deceive no one. It is as if the poet felt bound to say, "that the gods had taken the matter into their most serious consideration,"[1] "that it was with great regret that the gods found themselves unable to concede a longer term of existence to the Daunian hero,"[2] while all the time he was well aware that the gods had never been consulted in the matter at all.

And even that more real and comprehensive religion of Rome, the inspiring belief in the destinies of the Eternal City, lacked that which is lacking to all such religions, whether their object be one city

[1] A. xii. 843.        [2] A. xii. 725.

only or the whole corporate commonwealth of men.
There was no place in it for individual recompense;
it left unanswered the imperious demand of the
moral sense that not one sentient soul shall be
created to agony that others may be blest.  Such
faiths may inspire ceremonial, may prompt to action,
but they cannot justify the ways of God to man, nor
satisfy or control the heart.

It is well known that in the central passage of
the Æneid, the speech of the shade of Anchises to
Æneas in Elysium,[1] Virgil has abruptly relinquished
his efforts to revive or harmonise legendary beliefs,
and has propounded an answer to the riddle of the
universe in an unexpectedly definite form.  It would
be interesting to trace the elements of Stoic, Platonic,
Pythagorean thought which combine in this remarkable passage.   But such an inquiry would be beyond
our present scope, and must in any case rest largely
upon conjecture, for Virgil, who seems to have been
working upon this exposition till the last,[2] and who
meant, as we know, to devote to philosophy the rest
of his life after the completion of the Æneid, has
given us no indication of the process by which he
reached these results—results singular as contrasting
so widely with the official religion of which he was
in some sort the representative, yet which may

[1] A. vi. 724-755.
[2] See A. vi. 743-7, as indicating that the arrangement of this
passage is incomplete.

surprise us less when we consider their close coincidence with the independent conclusions of many
thinkers of ancient and modern times.    A brief
description of the passage referred to will fitly conclude the present essay.

Æneas, warned of Anchises in a vision, has
penetrated the underworld to consult his father's
shade.    He finds Anchises surrounded by an in-
numerable multitude of souls, who congregate on
Lethe's shore.    His father tells him that these souls
are drinking the waters of oblivion, and will then
return to live again on earth.    Æneas is astonished
at this, and the form of the question which he
asks[1] is in itself highly significant.    Compared, for
example, with the famous contrast which the
Homeric Achilles draws between even the poorest
life on happy earth and the forlorn kingship of the
shades, it indicates that a change has taken place
which of all speculative changes is perhaps the most
important, that the ideal has been shifted from the
visible to the invisible, from the material to the
spiritual world—

"O father, must I deem that souls can pray
   Hence to turn backward to the worldly day?
   Change for that weight of flesh these forms more fair,
   For that sun's sheen this paradisal air?"

The speech of Anchises in answer is in a certain
sense the most Virgilian passage in Virgil.    All his

[1] A. vi. 719.

characteristics appear in it in their highest intensity; the pregnant allusiveness, the oracular concentration, the profound complexity, and through them all that unearthly march of song, that " Elysian beauty, melancholy grace," which made him the one fit master for that other soul whom he " *mise dentro alle segrete cose*," to whom in face of purgatory's fiercest fire[1] he promised the reward of constancy, and spoke of the redemptions of love.

The translator may well hesitate before such a passage as this. But as a knowledge of the Theodicy here unfolded is absolutely necessary to the English reader who would understand Virgil aright, some version shall be given here—

" One Life through all the immense creation runs,
One Spirit is the moon's, the sea's, the sun's;
All forms in the air that fly, on the earth that creep,
And the unknown nameless monsters of the deep,—
Each breathing thing obeys one Mind's control,
And in all substance is a single Soul.
First to each seed a fiery force is given;
And every creature was begot in heaven;
Only their flight must hateful flesh delay
And gross limbs moribund and cumbering clay.
So from that hindering prison and night forlorn
Thy hopes and fears, thy joys and woes are born,
Who only seest, till death dispart thy gloom,
The true world glow through crannies of a tomb.

---

[1] Purg. xxvii. 20

Nor all at once thine ancient ills decay,
Nor quite with death thy plagues are purged away ;
In wondrous wise hath the iron entered in,
And through and through thee is a stain of sin ;
Which yet again in wondrous wise must be
Cleansed of the fire, abolished ·in the sea ;
Ay, thro' and thro' that soul unclothed must go
Such spirit-winds as where they list will blow ; —
O hovering many an age ! for ages bare,
Void in the void and impotent in air !

Then, since his sins unshriven the sinner wait,
And to each soul that soul herself is Fate,
Few to heaven's many mansions straight are sped
(Past without blame that Judgment of the dead),
The most shall mourn till tarrying Time hath wrought
The extreme deliverance of the airy thought, —
Hath left unsoiled by fear or foul desire
The spirit's self, the elemental fire.

And last to Lethe's stream on the ordered day
These all God summoneth in great array ;
Who from that draught reborn, no more shall know
Memory of past or dread of destined woe,
But all shall there the ancient pain forgive,
Forget their life, and will again to live."

The shade of Anchises is silent here. But let us add some lines from the Georgics,[1] in which Virgil carries these souls yet farther, and to the term of their wondrous way—

" Then since from God those lesser lives began,
    And the eager spirits entered into man,

---

[1] G. iv. 223.

To God again the enfranchised soul must tend,
He is her home, her Author is her End ;
No death is hers ; when earthly eyes grow dim
Starlike she soars and Godlike melts in Him."

But why must we recur to an earlier poem for
the consummation which was most of all needed
here ? and why, at the end of the sixth book, has
the poet struck that last strange note of doubt and
discord, dismissing Æneas from the shades by the
deluding Ivory Gate, proclaiming, as it were, like
Plato, his Theodicy as " neither false nor true," as
a dream among dreams that wander and " visions
unbelievable and fair ?"   We turn, like Dante, in
hope of the wise guide's reply.   But he has left us
at last alone.[1]   He has led us to the region " where
of himself he can see no more ;"[2] we must expect
from him no longer " either word or sign."   He
parts from us in the " antelucan splendour," and at
the gate of heaven, at the very moment when a
hundred angels sing aloud with fuller meaning his
own words of solemn welcome and unforgetful love.[3]
To Dante all the glory of paradise could not avail to
keep his eyes from scorching tears at his " sweetest
father's " sad withdrawal and uncompleted way :—
we too, perhaps, may feel mournfully the lot of man
as we think of him on whose yearning spirit all
revelation that nature, or that science, or that faith

---

[1] Purg. xxx. 49.          [2] Purg. xxvii. 129, 139.
[3] Purg. xxx. 21.

could show, fell only as day's last glory on the
fading vision of the Carthaginian queen [1]—

" For thrice she turned, and thrice had fain dispread
    Her dying arms to lift her dying head ;
    Thrice in high heaven, with dimmed eyes wandering
        wide,
She sought the light, and found the light, and sighed."

So was it with those who by themselves should
not be made perfect ; they differed from the saints
of Christendom not so much in the emotion which
they offered as in the emotion with which they were
repaid ; it was elevation but it was not ecstasy ; it
came to them not as hope but as calm.    What
touch of unattainable holiness was lacking for their
reception into Dante's Paradisal Rose ? what ardour
of love was still unknown to them which should
have been their foretaste and their pledge of heaven ?
" Dark night enwraps their heads with hovering
gloom," and from this man, their solitary rearguard,
and on the very confines of the day, we can part
only in words of such sad reverence as salute in his
own song that last and most divinely glorified of the
inhabitants of the underworld [2]—

" Give, give me lilies ; thick the flowers be laid
    To greet that mighty, melancholy shade ;
    With such poor gifts let me his praise maintain,
And mourn with useless tears, and crown in vain."

[1] A. iv. 690.          [2] A. vi. 883.

# MARCUS AURELIUS ANTONINUS.

Ἄγου δέ μ', ὦ Ζεῦ, καὶ σύγ' ἡ Πεπρωμένη,
ὅποι ποθ'ὑμῖν ἐμὲ διατεταγμένος·
ὡς ἔψομαί γ' ἄοκνος· ἢν δὲ μὴ θέλω,
κακὸς γενόμενος οὐδὲν ἧττον ἔψομαι.
CLEANTHES.

SOME apology may seem to be due from one who ventures to treat once again of Marcus Aurelius Antoninus. Few characters in history have been oftener or more ably discussed during the present age, an age whose high aims and uncertain creed have found at once impulse and sympathy in the meditations of the crowned philosopher. And, finally, the most subtle and attractive of living historians has closed his strange portrait-gallery with this majestic figure, accounting that the sun of Christianity was not fully risen till it had seen the paling of the old world's last and purest star.

The subject has lost, no doubt, its literary freshness, but its moral and philosophical significance is still unexhausted. Even an increased interest, indeed, may be felt at the present time in considering

the relations which the philosophy of Marcus bears
either to ancient or to modern religious thought.
For he has been made, as it were, the saint and
exemplar of Agnosticism, the type of all such virtue and wisdom as modern criticism can allow to
be sound or permanent. It will be the object of
the following essay to suggest some reflections on
the position thus assigned to him, dwelling only
incidentally, and as briefly as may be consistent with
clearness, on the more familiar aspects of his opinions
and his career.

Character and circumstances, rather than talent or
originality, give to the thoughts of Marcus Aurelius
their especial value and charm. And although the
scanty notices of his life which have come down
to us have now been often repeated, it seems necessary to allude to some of the more characteristic of
them if we would understand the spiritual outlook
of one who is not a closet-philosopher moralising *in
vacuo*, but the son of Pius, the father of Commodus,
the master of a declining world.

The earliest statue which we know of Marcus
represents him as a youth offering sacrifice. The
earliest story of him, before his adoption into the
Imperial family, is of his initiation, at eight years
old, as a Salian priest of Mars, when the crowns
flung by the other priests fell here and there around
the recumbent statue, but the crown which young
Marcus threw to him lit and rested on the war-

god's head.   The boy-priest, we are told, could soon
conduct all the ceremonies of the Salian cult without
the usual prompter, for he served in all its offices,
and knew all its hymns by heart.   And it well became him thus to begin by exhibiting the characteristic piety of a child ;—who passes in his growing
years through the forms of worship, as of thought,
which have satisfied his remote forefathers, and
ripens himself for his adult philosophies with the
consecrated tradition of the past.

Our next glimpse is of the boy growing into
manhood in the household of his adopted father,
Antoninus Pius, whom he is already destined to
succeed on the Imperial throne.   One of the lessons
for which Marcus afterwards revered his father's
memory was the lesson of simplicity maintained in
the palace of princes, " far removed from the habits
of the rich."   The correspondence between the Imperial boy and his tutor, Fronto, shows us how pronounced this simplicity was, and casts a curious
side-light on the power of the Roman Emperor, who
can impress his own individuality with so uncom-
promising a hand not only on the affairs of the
empire, but on the personal habits of his court and
*entourage*.   In the modern world the more absolute
a monarch is in one way, the more is he in another
way fettered and constrained ; for his absolutism
relies on an artificial prestige which can dispense
with no means of impressing the vulgar mind.   And

in freer countries there is always a set of necessary persons, an habitual tone of manners, which the sovereign cannot afford to ignore. A George III. may lead a frugal family life, but he is forced to conciliate and consort with social leaders of habits quite opposite to his own. A William IV. who fails to do this adequately is pronounced to be " not in society." Antoninus Pius might certainly have been said to be "out of society," but that there was no society for him to be in except his own. The " optimates," whose opinion Cicero treats as the acknowledged standard— a group of notables enjoying social as well as official pre-eminence—had practically ceased to exist. Even the Senate, whose dignity the Antonines so sedulously cherished, consisted mainly of new and low-born men. Everything depended on the individual tastes of the ruler. Play-actors were at the head of society under Nero, spies under Domitian, philosophers under the Antonines.

The letters of the young Marcus to Fronto are very much such letters as might be written at the present day by the home-taught son of an English squire to a private tutor to whom he was much attached. They are, however, more effusive than an English style allows, and although Marcus in his youth was a successful athlete, they seldom refer to games or hunting. I translate one of them as a specimen of the rest :—

"I slept late this morning on account of my cold, but it is better. From five in the morning till

nine I partly read Cato on Agriculture, and partly
wrote, not quite such rubbish as yesterday. Then I
greeted my father, and then soothed my throat with
honey-water without absolutely gargling. Then I
attended my father as he offered sacrifice. Then to
breakfast. What do you think I ate? only a little
bread, though I saw the others devouring beans, onions,
and sardines! Then we went out to the vintage, and got
hot and merry, but left a few grapes still hanging, as
the old poet says, 'atop on the topmost bough.' At
noon we got home again; I worked a little, but it was
not much good. Then I chatted a long time with my
mother as she sat on her bed. My conversation consisted of, 'What do you suppose my Fronto is doing at
this moment?' to which she answered, 'And my Gratia,
what is she doing?' and then I, 'And our little birdie,
Gratia the less?' And while we were talking and
quarrelling as to which of us loved all of you the best,
the gong sounded, which meant that my father had gone
across to the bath. So we bathed and dined in the oil-
press room. I don't mean that we bathed in the press-
room; but we bathed and then dined, and amused
ourselves with listening to the peasants' banter. And
now that I am in my own room again, before I roll over
and snore, I am fulfilling my promise and giving an
account of my day to my dear tutor; and if I could
love him better than I do I would consent to miss him
even more than I miss him now. Take care of your-
self, my best and dearest Fronto, wherever you are.
The fact is that I love you, and you are far away."

Among the few hints which the correspondence
contains of the pupil's rank is one curiously charac-

teristic of his times and his destiny. Tutor and pupil, it seems, were in the habit of sending to each other "hypotheses," or imaginary cases, for the sake of practice in dealing with embarrassing circumstances as they arose. Marcus puts to Fronto the following "hard case" : "A Roman consul at the public games changes his consular dress for a gladiator's, and kills a lion in the amphitheatre before the assembled people. What is to be done to him ?" The puzzled Fronto contents himself with replying that such a thing could not possibly happen. But the boy's prevision was true. A generation later this very thing was done by a man who was not only a Roman consul, but a Roman Emperor, and the son of Marcus himself.

These were Marcus' happiest days. The companionship of Pius was a school of all the virtues. His domestic life with Faustina, if we are to believe contemporary letters rather than the scandal of the next century, was, at first at any rate, a model of happiness and peace. Marcus was already forty years old when Pius died. The nineteen years which remained to him were mainly occupied in driving back Germanic peoples from the northern frontiers of the empire. This labour was interrupted in A.D. 175 by the revolt of Avidius Cassius, an event which Marcus employed as a great occasion for magnanimity. The story is one which some dramatist might well seize upon, and show, with a

truer groundwork than Corneille in *Cinna*, how impossible is resentment to the philosophic soul.   But
the moment in these latter years which may be
selected as most characteristic was perhaps that of
the departure of Marcus to Germany in A.D. 178 for
his last and sternest war.   That great irruption of
the Marcomanni was compared by subsequent historians to the invasion of Hannibal.   It was in fact,
and it was dimly felt to be, the beginning of the
end.   The terrified Romans resorted to every expedi-
ent which could attract the favour of heaven or
fortify the spirit of man.   The Emperor threw a
blood-stained spear from the temple of Mars towards
the unknown North, invoking thus for the last time
in antique fashion the tutelary divinity of Rome.
The images of all the gods were laid on couches in
the sight of men, and that holy banquet was set
before them which constituted their worshippers'
most solemn appeal.   But no sacrifices henceforth
were to be for long effectual, nor omens favourable
again; they could only show the " Roman peace "
no longer sacred, the "Roman world " no longer
stretching "past the sun's year-long way," but
Janus' temple-doors for ever open, and Terminus
receding upon Rome.   Many new rites were also
performed, many foreign gods were approached with
strange expiations.   But the strangest feature in
this religious revival lay in an act of the Emperor
himself.   He was entreated, says Vulcatius, to give

a parting address to his subjects before he set out
into the wilderness of the north; and for three
days he expounded his philosophy to the people of
Rome.  The anecdote is a strange one, but hardly in
itself improbable.  It accords so well with Marcus'
trust in the power of reason, his belief in the duty
of laying the truth before men !   One can imagine
the sincere gaze, such as his coins show to us ; the
hand, as in the great equestrian statue of the Capitol, uplifted, as though to bless ; the countenance
controlled, as his biographers tell us, to exhibit
neither joy nor pain ; the voice and diction, not
loud nor striking, but grave and clear, as he bade
his hearers "reverence the dæmon within them,"
and "pass from one unselfish action to another,
with memory of God."   Like the fabled Arthur,
he was, as it were, the conscience amid the warring
passions of his knights ; like Arthur, he was himself going forth to meet "death, or he knew not
what mysterious doom."

For indeed his last years are lost in darkness.
A few anecdotes tell of his failing body and resolute
will ; a few bas-reliefs give in fragments a confused
story of the wilderness and of war.   We see marshes
and forests, bridges and battles, captive Sarmatians
brought to judgment, and Marcus still with his hand
uplifted as though bestowing pardon or grace.

The region in which these last years were spent
is to this day one of the most melancholy in Europe.

The forces of nature run to waste without use or
beauty.   The great Danube spreads himself languidly
between uncertain shores.   As it was in the days of
Marcus so is it now; the traveller from Vienna
eastward still sees the white mist cling to the desolate river-terraces, the clouds of wild-fowl swoop and
settle among the reedy islands, and along the bays
and promontories of the brimming stream.

But over these years hung a shadow darker than
could be cast by any visible foe.   Plague had become endemic in the Roman world.   The pestilence
brought from Asia by Verus in A.D. 166 had not
yet abated; it had destroyed already (as it would
seem) half the population of the Empire; it was
achieving its right to be considered by careful historians as the most terrible calamity which has ever
fallen upon men.   Destined, as it were, to sever race
from race and era from era, the plague struck its last
blow against the Roman people upon the person of
the Emperor himself.   He died in the camp, alone.
" Why weep for me," were his last words of stern
self-suppression, " and not think rather of the pestilence, and of the death of all ?"

When the news of his death reached Rome few
tears, we are told, were shed.   For it seemed to the
people that Marcus, like Marcellus, had been but
lent to the Roman race; it was natural that he
should pass back again from the wilderness to his
celestial home.   Before the official honours had been

paid to him the Senate and people by acclamation
at his funeral saluted him as " The Propitious God."
No one, says the chronicler, thought of him as
Emperor any more ; but the young men called on
" Marcus, my father," the men of middle age on
" Marcus, my brother," the old men on " Marcus,
my son." *Homo homini deus est, si suum officium
sciat*—and it may well be that those who thus honoured and thus lamented him had never known a
truer son or brother, father or god.

It does not fall within the scope of this essay to
enumerate in detail the measures by which Marcus
had earned the gratitude of the Empire.     But it is
important to remember that neither war nor philosophy had impaired his activity as an administrator.
Politically his reign, like that of Pius, was remarkable for his respectful treatment of the senatorial
order.     Instead of regarding senators as the natural
objects of imperial jealousy, or prey of imperial
avarice, he endeavoured by all means to raise their
dignity and consideration.     Some of them he employed as a kind of privy council, others as governors
of cities.     When at Rome he attended every meeting
of the Senate ; and even when absent in Campania
he would travel back expressly to be present at any
important debate ; nor did he ever leave the council-
hall till the sitting was adjourned.

While Marcus thus attempted to revive a respon-
sible upper class, he was far from neglecting the

interests of the poor. He developed the scheme
of state nurture and education for needy free-born
children which the Flavian emperors had begun.
He reformed the local government of Italy, and
made more careful provision against the recurring
danger of scarcity. He instituted the "tutelary
prætorship" which was to watch over the rights of
orphans — a class often unjustly treated at Rome.
And he fostered and supervised that great development of civil and criminal law which, under the
Antonines, was steadily giving protection to the
minor, justice to the woman, rights to the slave, and
transforming the stern maxims of Roman procedure
into a fit basis for the jurisprudence of the modern
world.

But indeed the true life and influence of Marcus
had scarcely yet begun. In his case, as in many
others, it was not the main occupation, the osten-
sible business of his life, which proved to have the
most enduring value. His most effective hours were
not those spent in his long adjudications, his cease-
less battles, his strenuous ordering of the concerns
of the Roman world. Rather they were the hours
of solitude and sadness, when, "among the Quadi,"
"on the Granua," "at Carnuntum," he consoled his
lonely spirit by jotting down in fragmentary sen-
tences the principles which were his guide through
life. The little volume was preserved by some for-
tunate accident. For many centuries it was accounted

as a kind of curiosity of literature—as heading the
brief list of the writings of kings. From time to
time some earnest spirit discovered that the help
given by the little book was of surer quality than
he could find in many a volume which promised
more. One and another student was moved to
translate it—from old Gataker of Rotherhithe, com-
pleting the work in his seventy-eighth year, as his
best preparation for death, to " Cardinal Francis
Barberini the elder, who dedicated the translation
to his soul, in order to make it redder than his
purple at the sight of the virtues of this Gentile." [1]
But the complete success of the book was reserved
for the present century. I will quote one passage
only as showing the position which it has taken
among some schools of modern thought—a passage
in which a writer celebrated for his nice distinctions
and balanced praise has spoken of the *Meditations*
in terms of more unmixed eulogy than he has ever
bestowed elsewhere :—

"Véritable Evangile éternel," says M. Renan, "le
livre des Pensées ne vieillira jamais, car il n'affirme
aucun dogme. L'Evangile a vieilli en certaines parties;
la science ne permet plus d'admettre la naïve conception du surnaturel qui en fait la base. Le surnaturel
n'est dans les Pensées qu'une petite tache insignifiante,
qui n'atteint pas la merveilleuse beauté du fond. La

---

[1] See the preface to Mr. Long's admirable translation. The
quotations from the *Meditations* in this essay are given partly in
Mr. Long's words.

science pourrait détruire Dieu et l'âme, que le livre des
Pensées resterait jeune encore de vie et de vérité.   La
religion de Marc-Aurèle, comme le fut par moments celle
de Jésus, est la religion absolue, celle qui résulte du
simple fait d'une haute conscience morale placée en face
de l'univers.   Elle n'est ni d'une race ni d'un pays.
Aucune révolution, aucun progrès, aucune découverte ne
pourront la changer."

What then, we may ask, and how attained to,
was the wisdom which is thus highly praised?
How came it that a man of little original power,
in an age of rhetoric and commonplace, was able
to rise to the height of so great an argument, and
to make of his most secret ponderings the religious
manual of a far-distant world?   This question can
scarcely be answered without a few preliminary reflections on the historical development of religion at
Rome.

Among all the civilised religions of antiquity
the Roman might well seem the least congenial
either to the beliefs or to the emotions of modern
times.   From the very first it bears all the marks
of a political origin.   When the antiquarian Varro
treats first of the state and then of the gods, " because in order that gods may be established states
must first exist," he is but retracing faithfully the
real genesis of the cult of Rome.   Composed of
elements borrowed from various quarters, it dealt
with all in a legal, external, unimaginative spirit.

The divination and ghost-religion, which it drew from the Etruscans and other primitive sources, survived in the state-augury and in the domestic worship of the Lares, only in a formal and half-hearted way. The nature-religion, which came from the Aryan forefathers of Rome, grew frigid indeed when it was imprisoned in the *Indigitamenta*, or Official Handy-book of the Gods. It is not to Rome, though it may often be to Italy, that the anthropologist must look for instances of those quaint rites which form in many countries the oldest existing links between civilised and primitive conceptions of the operations of an unseen Power. It is not from Rome that the poet must hope for fresh developments of those exquisite and unconscious allegories, which even in their most hackneyed reproduction still breathe on us the glory of the early world. The most enthusiastic of pagans or neo-pagans could scarcely reverence with much emotion the botanical accuracy of Nodotus, the god of Nodes, and Volutina, the goddess of Petioles, nor tremble before the terrors of Spiniensis and Robigus, the austere Powers of Blight and Brambles, nor eagerly implore the favour of Stercutius and Sterquilinus, the beneficent deities of Manure.[1]

This shadowy system of divinities is a mere

[1] Of some of these Powers it is hard to say whether they are to be considered as celestial or the reverse. Such are Carnea, the Goddess of Embonpoint, and Genius Portorii Publici, the Angel of Indirect Taxation.

elaboration of the primitive notion that religion
consists in getting whatever can be got from the
gods, and that this must be done by asking the
right personages in the proper terms.   The boast of
historian or poet that the old Romans were "most
religious mortals," or that they "surpassed in piety
the gods themselves," refers entirely to punctuality
of outward observance, considered as a definite *quid
pro quo* for the good things desired.   It is not hard
to be "more pious than the gods" if piety on our
part consists in asking decorously for what we
want, and piety on their part in immediately granting it.

It is plain that it was not, in this direction that
the Romans found a vent for the reverence and
the self-devotion in which their character was
assuredly not deficient.   Their true worship, their
true piety, were reserved for a more concrete,
though still a vast ideal.   As has been often said,
the religion of the Romans was Rome.   Her true
saints were her patriots, Curtius and Scævola,
Horatius, Regulus, Cato.   Her "heaven-descended
maxim" was not γνῶθι σεαυτὸν, but *Delenda est
Carthago*.   But a concrete idea must necessarily
lose in fixedness what it gains in actuality.   As
Rome became the Roman Empire the temper of her
religion must needs change with the fortunes of its
object.   While the fates of the city yet hung in
the balance the very thought of her had been

enough to make *Roman* for all ages a synonym for *heroic* virtue. But when a heterogeneous world-wide empire seemed to derive its unity from the Emperor's personality alone, men felt that the object of so many deeds of piety had disappeared through their very success. Devotion to Rome was transformed into the worship of Cæsar, and the one strain of vital religion which had run through the Commonwealth was stiffened like all the rest into a dead official routine.

Something better than this was needed for cultivated and serious men. To take one instance only, what was the Emperor himself to worship? It might be very well for obsequious provinces to erect statues to the *Indulgentia Cæsaris*. But Cæsar himself could hardly be expected to adore his own Good-humour. In epochs like these, when a national religion has lost its validity in thoughtful minds, and the nation is pausing, as it were, for further light, there is a fair field for all comers. There is an opportunity for those who wish either to eliminate the religious instinct, or to distort it, or to rationalise it, or to vivify; for the secularist and the charlatan, for the philosopher and the prophet. In Rome there was assuredly no lack of negation and indifference, of superstition and its inseparable fraud. But two streams of higher tendency rushed into the spiritual vacuum, two currents which represented, broadly speaking, the main religious and the main ethical tradition of mankind. The first of these, which we must pass by for the present, had its origin in the legendary Pythagoras and the remoter East. The second took the form of a generalised and simplified Stoicism.

Stoicism, of course, was no new thing in Rome. It had come in with Greek culture at the time of the Punic wars; it had commended itself by its proud precision to Roman habits of thought and life; it had been welcomed as a support for the state religion, a method of allegorising Olympus which yet might be accounted orthodox. The names of Cato and Brutus maintained the Stoic tradition through the death-throes of the Republic. But the stern independence of the Porch was not invoked to aid in the ceremonial revival with which Augustus would fain have renewed the old Roman virtue. It is among the horrors of Nero's reign that we find Stoicism taking its place as a main spiritual support of men. But as it becomes more efficacious it becomes also less distinctive. In Seneca, in Epictetus, most of all in Marcus himself, we see it gradually discarding its paradoxes, its controversies, its character as a specialised philosophical sect. We hear less of its logic, its cosmogony, its portrait of the ideal Sage. It insists rather on what may be termed the catholic verities of all philosophers, on the sole importance of virtue,

the spiritual oneness of the universe, the brotherhood of men.    From every point of view this latter
Stoicism afforded unusual advantages to the soul
which aimed at wisdom and virtue.    It was a philosophy; but by dint of time and trial it had run
itself clear of the extravagance and unreality of the
schools.    It was a reform; but its attitude towards
the established religion was at once friendly and
independent, so that it was neither cramped by
deference nor embittered by reaction.    Its doctrines
were old and true; yet it had about it a certain
freshness as being in fact the first free and medi-
tative outlook on the universe to which the Roman
people had attained.    And, more than all, it had
ready to its hand a large remainder of the most
famous store of self-devotedness that the world has
seen.    Stoicism was the heir of the old Roman
virtue; happy is the philosophy which can support
its own larger creed on the instincts of duty inherited from many a generation of narrow upright-
ness, of unquestioned law.

But the opportunity for the very flower of Stoic
excellence was due to the caprice of a great amateur.
Hadrian admired both beauty and virtue; his choice
of Antinous and of Marcus gave to the future world
the standard of the sculptor and the standard of
the moralist; the completest types of physical and
moral perfection which Roman history has handed
down.    And yet among the names of his bene-

factors with which the scrupulous gratitude of
Marcus has opened his self-communings, the name
*Hadrianus* does not occur.  The boy thus raised
to empire has passed by Hadrian, who gave him
all the kingdoms of the world and the glory of
them, for Severus, who taught him to disdain them
all.

Among all the *Meditations* none is at once more
simple and more original than this exordium of
thanksgiving.  It is the single-hearted utterance of
a soul which knows neither desire nor pride, which
considers nothing as gain in her life's journey except the love of those souls who have loved her,——
the memory of those who have fortified her by the
spectacle and communication of virtue.

The thoughts that follow on this prelude are by
no means of an exclusively Stoic type.  They are
both more emotional and more agnostic than would
have satisfied Chrysippus or Zeno.  They are not
conceived in that tone of certainty and conviction
in which men lecture or preach, but with those sad
reserves, those varying moods of hope and despondency, which are natural to a man's secret ponderings
on the riddle of the world.  Even the fundamental
Stoic belief in God and Providence is not beyond
question in Marcus' eyes.  The passages where he
repeats the alternative " either gods or atoms " are
too strongly expressed to allow us to think that the
antithesis is only a trick of style.

" Either confusion and entanglement and scattering again: or unity, order, providence.   If the first case be, why do I wish to live amid the clashings of chance and chaos? or care for aught else but to become earth myself at last? and why am I disturbed, since this dispersion will come whatever I do? but if the latter case be the true one, I reverence and stand firm, and trust in him who rules.

" Thus wags the world, up and down, from age to age.   And either the universal mind determines each event; and if so, accept then that which it determines; or it has ordered once for all, and the rest follows in sequence; or indivisible elements are the origin of all things.   In a word, if there be a god, then all is well; if all things go at random, act not at random thou."

And along with this speculative openness, so much more sympathetic to the modern reader than the rhetoric of Seneca or even the lofty dogmatism of Epictetus, there is a total absence of the Stoic pride.   His self-reverence is of that truest kind which is based on a man's conception not of what he is, but of what he ought to be.

" Men cannot admire the sharpness of thy wits.   Be it so; but many other things there are of which thou canst not say, I was not formed for them.   Show those things which are wholly in thy power to show: sincerity, dignity, laboriousness, self-denial, contentment, frugality, kindliness, frankness, simplicity, seriousness, magnanimity.   Seest thou not how many things there are in which, with no excuse of natural incapacity, thou voluntarily fallest short? or art thou compelled by defect of nature

to murmur and be stingy and flatter and complain of
thy poor body, and cajole and boast, and disquiet thyself in vain ?   No, by the gods ! but of all these things
thou mightest have been rid long ago.   Nay, if indeed
thou be somewhat slow and dull of comprehension, thou
must exert thyself about this too, and not neglect it nor
be contented with thy dulness."

Words like these, perhaps, exalt human nature
in our eyes quite as highly as if we had heard Marcus insisting, like some others of his school, that
"the sage is as useful to Zeus as Zeus to him," or
that "courage is more creditable to sages than it is
to gods, since gods have it by nature, but sages by
practice."

And having thus overheard his self-communings,
with what a sense of soundness and reality do we
turn to the steady fervour of his constantly repeated
ideal !

"Let the god within thee be the guardian of a living
being, masculine, adult, political, and a Roman, and a
ruler ; who has taken up his post in life as one that
awaits with readiness the signal that shall summon him
away. . . . And such a man, who delays no longer to
strive to be in the number of the best, is as a priest and
servant of the gods, obeying that god who is in himself
enshrined, who renders him unsoiled of pleasure, un-
harmed by any pain, untouched by insult, feeling no
wrong, a wrestler in the noblest struggle, which is, that
by no passion he may be overthrown ; dyed to the depth
in justice, and with his whole heart welcoming whatsoever cometh to him and is ordained."

The ideal is sketched on Stoic lines, but the writer's temperament is not cast in the old Stoic mould.   He reminds us rather of modern sensitiveness, in his shrinking from the presence of coarse and selfish persons, and in his desire, obvious enough but constantly checked, for the sympathy and approbation of those with whom he lived.   The self-sufficing aspect of Stoicism has in him lost all its exclusiveness; it is represented only by the resolute recurrence to conscience as the one support against the buffets of the world.

"I do my duty; other things trouble me not; for either they are things without life, or things without reason, or things that have wandered and know not the way."

And thus, while all the dealings of Marcus with his fellow-men are summed up in the two endeavours —to imitate their virtues, and to amend, or at least patiently to endure, their defects—it is pretty plain which of these two efforts was most frequently needed.   His fragmentary thoughts present us with a long series of struggles to rise from the mood of disgust and depression into the mood of serene benevolence, by dwelling strongly on a few guiding lines of self-admonition.

"Begin the morning by saying to thyself: I shall meet with the busybody, the ungrateful, arrogant, deceitful, envious, unsocial.   All these things happen to them by reason of their ignorance of what is good and evil. But I who have seen the nature of the good that it is beautiful, and of the bad that it is ugly, and the nature of him who sins, that it is akin to mine, and participates in the same divinity, I can neither be injured by any of them, for no man can fix a foulness on me; nor can I be angry nor hate my brother."

There is reason, indeed, to fear that Marcus loved his enemies too well; that he was too much given to blessing those that cursed him. It is to him, rather than to any Christian potentate, that we must look for an example of the dangers of applying the gospel maxims too unreservedly to the business of the turbid world. For indeed the practical danger lies not in the overt adoption of those counsels of an ideal mildness and mercy, but even in the mere attainment of a temper so calm and lofty that the promptings of vanity or anger are felt no more. The task of curbing and punishing other men, of humiliating their arrogance, exposing their falsity, upbraiding their sloth, is in itself so distasteful, when there is no personal rivalry or resentment to prompt it, that it is sure to be performed too gently, or neglected for more congenial duties. Avidius Cassius, burning his disorderly soldiers alive to gain himself a reputation for vigour, was more comprehensible to the mass of men, more immediately efficacious, than Marcus representing to the selfish and wayward Commodus "that even bees did not act in such a manner, nor any of those creatures which live in troops."

But the very incongruity between the duties which Marcus was called on to perform and the spirit which he brought to their performance, the fate which made him by nature a sage and a saint, by profession a ruler and a warrior, all this gave to his character a dignity and a completeness which it could scarcely otherwise have attained. The master of the world more than other men might feel himself bound to "live as on a mountain;" he whose look was life or death to millions might best set the example of the single-heartedness which need hide the thought of no waking moment from any one's knowledge,—till a man's eyes should reveal all that passed within him, "even as there is no veil upon a star." The Stoic philosophy which required that the sage should be indifferent to worldly goods found its crowning exemplar in a sage who possessed them all.

And, indeed, in the case of Marcus the difficulty was not to disdain the things of earth, but to care for them enough. The touch of Cynic crudity with which he analyses such things as men desire, reminds us sometimes of those scornful pictures of secular life which have been penned in the cloister. For that indifference to transitory things which has often made the religious fanatic the worst of citizens is not the danger of the fanatic alone. It is a part also of the melancholy of the magnanimous; of the mood when the "joy and gladness" which the Stoics promised to their sage die down in the midst of "such darkness and dirt," as Marcus calls it, "that it is hard to imagine what there is which is worthy to be prized highly, or seriously pursued."

Nay, it seems to him that even if, in Plato's phrase, he could become "the spectator of all time and of all existence," there would be nothing in the sight to stir the exultation, to change the solitude of the sage. The universe is full of living creatures, but there is none of them whose existence is so glorious and blessed that by itself it can justify all other Being; the worlds are destroyed and re-created with an endless renewal, but they are tending to no world more pure than themselves; they are not even, as in Hindoo myth, ripening in a secular expectancy till Buddha come; they are but repeating the same littlenesses from the depth to the height of heaven, and reiterating throughout all eternity the fears and follies of a day.

"If thou wert lifted on high and didst behold the manifold fates of men; and didst discern at once all creatures that dwell round about him, in the ether and the air; then howso oft thou thus wert raised on high, these same things thou shouldst ever see, all things alike, and all things perishing. And where is, then, the glory?"

Men who look out on the world with a gaze thus disenchanted are apt to wrap themselves in a cynical indifference or in a pessimistic despair. But character is stronger than creed; and Marcus carries into the midst of the saddest surroundings his nature's imperious craving to reverence and to love. He feels, indeed, that the one joy which could have attached him to the world is wholly wanting to him.

"This is the only thing, if anything there be, which could have drawn thee backwards and held thee still in life, if it had been granted thee to live with men of like principles with thyself. But now thou seest how great a pain there is in the discordance of thy life with other men's, so that thou sayest: Come quick, O death! lest perchance I too should forget myself."

Nor can he take comfort from any steadfast hope of future fellowship with kindred souls.

"How can it be that the gods, having ordered all things rightly and with good-will towards men, have overlooked this thing alone: that some men, virtuous indeed, who have as it were made many a covenant with heaven, and through holy deeds and worship have had closest communion with the divine, that these men, when once they are dead, should not live again, but be extinguished for ever? Yet if this be so, be sure that if it ought to have been otherwise the gods would have done it. For were it just, it would also be possible; were it according to nature, nature would have had it so."

For thus he believes without proof and without argument that all is for the best; that everything which happens is for the advantage of every constituent life in nature, since everything is for the advantage of the whole. He will not entertain the idea that the Powers above him may be not all-

powerful; or the Wisdom which rules the universe
less than all-wise.   And this optimism comes from
no natural buoyancy of temper.   There is scarcely
a trace in the *Meditations* of any mood of careless
joy.   He never rises beyond the august contentment
of the man who accepts his fate.

"All things are harmonious to me which are harmonious to thee, O Universe.   Nothing for me is too
early nor too late which is in due time for thee.   All is
fruit to me which thy seasons, O Nature, bear.   From
thee are all things, and in thee all, and all return to
thee.   The poet says, 'Dear city of Cecrops;' shall I
not say, 'Dear city of God?'"

There have been many who, with no more belief
than Marcus in a personal immortality, have striven,
like him, to accept willingly the world in which they
found themselves placed.   But sometimes they have
marred the dignity of their position by attempting
too eagerly to find a reason for gladness; they have
dwelt with exultation upon a terrene future for our
race from which Marcus would still have turned
and asked, "Where, then, is the glory?"   It would
have seemed to him that a triumphant tone like
this can only come from the soilure of philosophy
with something of the modern spirit of industrial
materialism and facile enjoyment; he would have
preferred that his own sereneness should be less near
to complacency than to resignation; he would still
have chosen the temper of that saintly Stoic, whose

rude, strong verses break in with so stern a piety
among the fragments of philosophic Greece :—

"Lead, lead Cleanthes, Zeus and holy Fate,
   Where'er ye place my post, to serve or wait :
   Willing I follow ; were it not my will,
   A baffled rebel I must follow still."

These, however, are differences only of tone and
temper overlying what forms in reality a vast body
of practical agreement.   For the scheme of thought
and belief which has thus been briefly sketched is
not only in itself a noble and a just one.   It is a
kind of common creed of wise men, from which all
other views may well seem mere deflections on the
side of an unwarranted credulity or of an exaggerated
despair.   Here, it may be not unreasonably urged,
is the moral backbone of all universal religions ; and
as civilisation has advanced, the practical creed of
all parties, whatever their speculative pretensions,
has approximated ever more nearly to these plain
principles and uncertain hopes.

This view of the tendency of religious progress
is undoubtedly the simplest and most plausible which
history presents to the philosopher who is not himself pledged to the defence of any one form of what
is termed supernatural belief.   But it has to contend
with grave difficulties of historical fact ; and among
these difficulties the age of the Antonines presents
one of the most considerable.   Never had the ground

been cleared on so large a scale for pure philosophy; never was there so little external pressure exerted in favour of any traditional faith. The persecutions of the Christians were undertaken on political and moral, rather than on theological grounds; they were the expression of the feeling with which a modern State might regard a set of men who were at once Mormons and Nihilists——refusing the legal tokens of respect to constituted authorities, while suspected of indulging in low immorality at the bidding of an ignorant superstition. And yet the result of this age of tolerance and enlightenment was the gradual recrudescence, among the cultivated as well as the ignorant, of the belief in a perceptible interaction of the seen and the unseen world, culminating at last in the very form of that belief which had shown itself most resolute, most thoroughgoing, and most intractable.

For the triumph of Christianity in the Roman Empire must not be looked upon as an anomalous or an isolated phenomenon. It was rather the triumph along the whole line, though (as is usual in great triumphs) in an unlooked-for fashion, of a current of tendency which had coexisted obscurely with State-religion, patriotism, and philosophy, almost from the first beginnings of the city. The anomaly, if there were one, consisted in the fact that the hints and elements of this new power, which was destined to be the second life of Rome, were to be found, not

in the time-honoured ordinances of her Senate, or
the sober wisdom of her schools, but in the fanaticism
of ignorant enthusiasts, in the dreams of a mystic
poet, in the alleged, but derided, experiences of a
few eccentric philosophers.   The introduction of
Christianity at Rome was the work not only of
Peter and Paul, but of Virgil and Varro.

For amidst the various creeds and philosophies,
by aid of which men have ordered their life on earth,
the most persistent and fundamental line of division is
surely this :—The question whether that life is to be
ordered by rules drawn from its own experience alone,
or whether there are indications which may justly
modify our conduct or expectations by some influx
of inspiration, or some phenomena testifying to the
existence of an unseen world, or to our continued
life after the body's decay ?   The instincts which
prompt to this latter view found, as has been already
implied, but little sustenance in the established cult
of Rome.   They were forced to satisfy themselves
in a fitful and irregular fashion by Greek and Oriental modes of religious excitement.   What sense
of elevation or reality may have been present to the
partakers in these alien enthusiasms we are not now
able to say.   The worships of Bacchus and Cybele
have been described to us by historians of the same
conservative temper as those who afterwards made
" an execrable superstition " of the worship of Christ.

Some scattered indications seem to imply a substratum of religious emotion, or of theurgic experiment, more extensive than the ordinary authorities have cared to record.  The proud and gay Catullus rises to his masterpiece in the description of that alternation of reckless fanaticism and sick recoil which formed throughout the so-called Ages of Faith the standing tragedy of the cloister.  More startling still is the story which shows us a group of the greatest personages of Rome in the last century before Christ, Nigidius Figulus, Appius Claudius, Publius Vatinius, Marcus Varro, subjected to police supervision on account of their alleged practice of summoning into visible presence the spirits of the dead.  "The whole system," says Professor Mommsen, "obtained its consecration—political, religious, and national—from the name of Pythagoras, the ultra-conservative statesman, whose supreme principle was 'to promote order and to check disorder,' the miracle-worker and necromancer, the primeval sage who was a native of Italy, who was interwoven even with the legendary history of Rome, and whose statue was to be seen in the Roman Forum."  This story might seem an isolated one but for one remarkable literary parallel.  In Virgil—perhaps the only Roman writer who possessed what would now be termed religious originality—we observe the co-existence of three separate lines of religious thought. There is the conservatism which loses no opportunity of enforcing the traditional worships of Rome, in

accordance at once with the poet's own temper of
mind, and with the plan of Augustus' ethical reforms.
There is the new fusion of the worship of Rome
with the worship of the Emperor—the only symbol
of spiritual unity between remote provincials and
the imperial city.   But finally, in the central passage
of his greatest poem, we come on a Pythagorean
creed, expressed, indeed, with some confusion and
hesitancy, but with earnest conviction and power,
and forming, as the well-known fragment of correspondence plainly implies, the dominant pre-occupation of the poet's later life.

Such a scheme, indeed, as the Pythagorean, with
its insistence on a personal immortality, and its
moral retribution adjusted by means of successive
existences with a greater nicety than has been employed by any other creed—such a scheme, if once
established, might have satisfied the spiritual needs of
the Roman world more profoundly and permanently
than either the worship of Jove or the worship of
Cæsar.   But it was not established.   The reasoning,
or the evidence, which had impressed Virgil, or the
group of philosophers, was not set forth before the
mass of men ; those instincts which we should now
term specifically religious remained unguided ; and
during the next three centuries we observe the love
of the marvellous and the supernatural dissociating
itself more and more from any ethical dogma.   There
are, no doubt, remarkable instances in these centuries

of an almost modern spirit of piety associated (as for instance in Apuleius) with the most bizarre religious vagaries. But on the whole the two worships which, until the triumph of Christianity, seemed most likely to overrun the civilised world were the worship of Mithra and the worship of Serapis. Now the name of Mithra can hardly be connected with moral conceptions of any kind. And the nearest that we can get to the character of Serapis is the fact that he was by many persons considered to be identical either with the principle of good or with the principle of evil.

Among these confused and one-sided faiths Christianity had an unique superiority. It was the only formulated and intelligible creed which united the two elements most necessary for a widely-received religion, namely, a lofty moral code, and the attestation of some actual intercourse between the visible and the invisible worlds.

It was not the morality of the Gospels alone which exercised the attractive force. Still less was it the speculations of Pauline theology, the high conceptions which a later age hardened into so immutable a system. It was the fact that this lofty teaching was based on beliefs which almost all men held already; that exhortations, nobler than those of Plutarch or Marcus, were supported by marvels better attested than those of Alexander of Abonoteichos, or Apollonius of Tyana. In a thousand ways, and by a thousand channels, the old faiths melted into the new. It was not only that such apologists as Justin and Minucius Felix were fond of showing that Christianity was, as it were, the crown of philosophy, the consummation of Platonic truth. More important was the fact that the rank and file of Christian converts looked on the universe with the same eyes as the heathens around them. All that they asked of these was to believe that the dimly-realised deities, whom the heathens regarded rather with fear than love, were in reality powers of evil; while above the Oriental additions so often made to their Pantheon was to be superposed one ultimate divinity, alone beneficent, and alone to be adored.

The hierarchy of an unseen universe must needs be a somewhat shadowy and arbitrary thing. To those, indeed, whose imagination is already exercised on such matters a new scheme of the celestial powers may come with an acceptable sense of increasing insight into the deep things of God. But in one who, like Marcus, has learnt to believe that in such matters the truest wisdom is to recognise that we cannot know, in him a scheme like the Christian is apt to inspire incredulity by its very promise of completeness,—suspicion by the very nature of the evidence which is alleged in its support.

Neither the Stoic school in general, indeed, nor Marcus himself, were clear of all superstitious tendency. The early masters of the sect had pushed their doctrine of the solidarity of all things to the point of anticipating that the liver of a particular bullock, itself selected from among its fellows by some mysterious fitness of things, might reasonably give an indication of the result of an impending battle. When it was urged that on this principle everything might be expected to be indicative of everything else, the Stoics answered that so it was, but that only when such indications lay in the liver could we understand them aright. When asked how we came to understand them when thus located, the Stoic doctors seem to have made no sufficient reply. We need not suppose that Marcus participated in absurdities like these. He himself makes no assertion of this hazardous kind, except only that remedies for his ailments " have been shown to him in dreams." And this is not insisted on in detail; it rather forms part of that habitual feeling or impression which, if indeed it be superstitious, is yet a superstition from which no devout mind, perhaps, was ever wholly free; namely, that he is the object of a special care and benevolence proceeding from some holy power. Such a feeling implies no belief either in merit or in privilege beyond that of other men; but just as the man who is strongly willing, though it be proved to him that his choice is determined by his antecedents, must yet feel assured that he can deflect its issue this way or that, even so a man, the habit of whose soul is worship, cannot but see at least a reflection of his own virtue in the arch of heaven, and bathe his spirit in the mirage projected from the well-spring of its own love.

For such an instinct, for all the highest instincts of his heart, Marcus would no doubt have found in Christianity a new and full satisfaction. The question, however, whether he ought to have become a Christian is not worth serious discussion. In the then state of belief in the Roman world it would have been as impossible for a Roman Emperor to become a Christian as it would be at the present day for a Czar of Russia to become a Buddhist. Some Christian apologists complain that Marcus was not converted by the miracle of the " Thundering Legion." They forget that though some obscure persons may have ascribed that happy occurrence to Christian prayers, the Emperor was assured on much higher authority that he had performed the miracle himself. Marcus, indeed, would assuredly not have insisted on his own divinity. He would not have been deterred by any Stoic exclusiveness from incorporating in his scheme of belief, already infiltrated with Platonic thought, such elements as those apologists who start from St. Paul's speech at Athens would have urged him to introduce. But an acceptance of the new faith involved much more than this. It involved tenets which might well seem to be a mere reversion to the world-old superstitions and sorceries of barbarous tribes. Such alleged phenomena as those of possession, inspiration, healing by imposition of hands, luminous appearances, modification and movement of material objects, formed, not, as some later apologists would have it, a mere accidental admixture, but an essential and loudly-asserted element in the new religion. The apparition of its Founder after death was its very *raison d'être* and triumphant demonstration. The Christian advocate may say indeed with reason, that phenomena such as these, however suspicious the associations which they might invoke, however primitive the stratum of belief to which they might seem at first to degrade the disciple, should nevertheless have been examined afresh on their own evidence, and would have been found to be supported by a consensus of testimony which has since then overcome the world. Addressed to an age in which Reason was supreme, such arguments might have carried convincing weight. But mankind had certainly not reached a point in the age of the Antonines,—if indeed we have reached it yet,—at which the recollections of barbarism were cast into so remote a background that the leaders of civilised thought could lightly reopen questions the closing of which might seem to have marked a clear advance along the path of enlightenment. It is true, indeed, that the path of enlightenment is not a royal road but a labyrinth; and that those who have marched too unhesitatingly in one direction have generally been obliged to retrace their steps, to unravel some forgotten clue, to explore some turning which they had already passed by. But the practical rulers of men must not take the paths which seem to point backwards until they hear in front of them the call of those who have chosen that less inviting way.

An emperor who had "learnt from Diognetus not to give credit to what is said by miracle-workers and jugglers about incantations and the driving away of demons and such things," might well feel that so much as to inquire into the Gospel stories would be a blasphemy against his philosophic creed. Even the heroism of Christian martyrdom left him cold. In words which have become proverbial as a wise man's mistake, he stigmatises the Christian contempt of death as "sheer party spirit." And yet——it is an old thought, but it is impossible not to recur to it once more——what might he not have learnt from these despised sectaries! the melancholy Emperor from Potheinus and Blandina, smiling on the rack!

Of the Christian virtues, it was not *faith* which was lacking to him. His faith indeed was not that bastard faith of theologians, which is nothing more than a willingness to assent to historical propositions on insufficient evidence. But it was faith such as Christ demanded of His disciples, the steadfastness of the soul in clinging, spite of doubts, of difficulties, even of despair, to whatever she has known of best; the resolution to stand or fall by the noblest hypothesis. To Marcus the alternative of "gods or

atoms "—of a universe ruled either by blind chance
or by an intelligent Providence—was ever present
and ever unsolved; but in action he ignored that ·
dark possibility, and lived as a member of a sacred
cosmos, and co-operant with ordering gods.

Again, it might seem unjust to say that he was
wanting in love.  No one has expressed with more
conviction the interdependence and kinship of men.

"We are made to work together, like feet, like hands,
like eyelids, like the rows of the upper and lower teeth."
"It is peculiar to man to love even those who do wrong ;
and thou wilt love them if, when they err, thou bethink
thee that they are to thee near akin."   "Men exist for
the sake of one another ; teach them then, or bear with
them."   "When men blame thee, or hate thee, or revile
thee, pass inward to their souls ; see what they are.
Thou wilt see that thou needst not trouble thyself as to
what such men think of thee.   And thou must be kindly
affectioned to them ; for by nature they are friends ;
and the gods, too, help and answer them in many ways."
"Love men, and love them from the heart."   " 'Earth
loves the shower,' and ' sacred æther loves ;' and the
whole universe loves the making of that which is to be.
I say then to the universe : Even I, too, love as thou."

And yet about the love of a John, a Paul, a
Peter, there is the ring of a note which is missing
here.  Stoic love is but an injunction of reason and
a means to virtue ; Christian love is the open secret
of the universe, and in itself the end of all.   In all
that wisdom can teach herein, Stoic and Christian

are at one. They both know that if a man would save his life he must lose it; that the disappearance of all selfish aims or pleasures in the universal life is the only pathway to peace. All religions that are worth the name have felt the need of this inward change; the difference lies rather in the light under which they regard it. To the Stoic in the West, as to the Buddhist in the East, it presented itself as a renunciation which became a deliverance, a tranquillity which passed into an annihilation. The Christian, too, recognised in the renunciation of the world a deliverance from its evil. But his spirit in those early days was occupied less with what he was resigning than with what he gained; the love of Christ constrained him; he died to self to find, even here on earth, that he had passed not into nothingness, but into heaven. In his eyes the Stoic doctrine was not false, but partly rudimentary and partly needless. His only objection, if objection it could be called, to the Stoic manner of facing the reality of the universe, was that the reality of the universe was so infinitely better than the Stoic supposed.

If, then, the Stoic love beside the Christian was "as moonlight unto sunlight, and as water unto wine," it was not only because the Stoic philosophy prescribed the curbing and checking of those natural emotions which Christianity at once guided and intensified by her new ideal. It was because the love

of Christ which the Christian felt was not a labori-
ous duty, but a self-renewing, self-intensifying force;
a feeling offered as to one who for ever responded
to it, as to one whose triumphant immortality had
brought his disciples' immortality to light.

So completely had the appearance of Jesus to
the faithful after his apparent death altered in
their eyes the aspect of the world.  So decisive
was the settlement of the old alternative, " Either
Providence or atoms," which was effected by the
firm conviction of a single spirit's beneficent return
along that silent and shadowy way.  So powerful a
reinforcement to Faith and Love was afforded by
the third of the Christian trinity of virtues—by the
grace of Hope.

But we are treading here on controverted ground.
It is not only that this great prospect has not yet
taken its place among admitted certainties; that
the hope and resurrection of the dead are still called
in question.  Much more than this; the most advanced school of modern moralists tends rather to
deny that "a sure and certain hope" in this matter
is to be desired at all.  Virtue, it is alleged, must
needs lose her disinterestedness if the solution of
the great problem were opened to her gaze.

" Pour nous," says M. Renan, who draws this moral
especially from the noble disinterestedness of Marcus
himself: "pour nous, on nous annoncerait un argument
péremptoire en ce genre, que nous ferions comme Saint

Louis, quand on lui parla de l'hostie miraculeuse ; nous refuserions d'aller voir.  Qu'avons nous besoin de ces preuves brutales, qui n'ont d'application que dans l'ordre grossier des faits, et qui gêneraient notre liberté ?"

This seems a strong argument; and if it be accepted it is practically decisive of the question at issue,——I do not say only between Stoicism and Christianity, but between all those systems which do not seek, and those which do seek, a spiritual communion for man external to his own soul, a spiritual continuance external to his own body.   If a proof of a beneficent Providence or of a future life be a thing to be deprecated, it will be indiscreet, or even immoral, to inquire whether such proof has been, or can be, obtained.   The world must stand with Marcus ; and there will be no extravagance in M. Renan's estimate of the Stoic morality as a sounder and more permanent system than that of Jesus Himself.

But generalisations like this demand a close examination.   Is the antithesis between interested and disinterested virtue a clear and fundamental one for all stages of spiritual progress?   Or may we not find that the conditions of the experiment vary, as it were, as virtue passes through different temperatures ; that our formula gives a positive result at one point, a negative at another, and becomes altogether unmeaning at a third?

It will be allowed, in the first place, that for an

indefinite time to come, and until the mass of mankind has advanced much higher above the savage
level than is as yet the case, it will be premature
to be too fastidious as to the beliefs which prompt
them to virtue. The first object is to give them
habits of self-restraint and well-doing, and we may
be well content if their crude notions of an unseen
Power are such as to reinforce the somewhat obscure
indications which life on earth at present affords
that honesty and truth and mercy bring a real
reward to men. But let us pass on to the extreme
-hypothesis on which the repudiation of any spiritual
help for man outside himself must ultimately rest.
Let us suppose that man's impulses have become
harmonised with his environment; that his tendency
to anger has been minimised by long-standing
gentleness; his tendency to covetousness by diffused
well-being; his tendency to sensuality by the increased preponderance of his intellectual nature.
How will the test of his disinterestedness operate
then? Why, it will be no more possible then for
a sane man to be deliberately wicked than it is possible now for a civilised man to be deliberately filthy
in his personal habits. We do not wish now that
it were uncertain whether filth were unhealthy in
order that we might be the more meritorious in
preferring to be clean. And whether our remote
descendants have become convinced of the reality
of a future life or no, it will assuredly never occur

to them that, without it, there might be a question whether virtue was a remunerative object of pursuit. Lapses from virtue there may still be in plenty; but inherited instinct will have made it inconceivable that a man should voluntarily be what Marcus calls a "boil or imposthume upon the universe," an island of selfishness in the mid-sea of sympathetic joy.

It is true, indeed, that in the present age, and for certain individuals, that choice of which M. Renan speaks has a terrible, a priceless reality. Many a living memory records some crisis when one who had rejected as unproved the traditional sanctions was forced to face the question whether his virtue had any sanction which still could stand; some night when the foundations of the soul's deep were broken up, and she asked herself why she still should cleave to the law of other men rather than to some kindlier monition of her own :—

> "Doch alles was dazu mich trieb,
> Gott, war so gut! ach, war so lieb!"

To be the conqueror in such a contest is the characteristic privilege of a time of transition like our own. But it is not the only, nor even the highest conceivable, form of virtue. It is an incident in the moral life of the individual; its possibility may be but an incident in the moral life of the race. It is but driving the enemy off the ground on which we wish to build our temple; there may be far greater trials of strength, endurance, courage, before we have raised its dome in air.

For after all it is only in the lower stages of ethical progress that to see the right is easy and to decide on doing it is hard. The time comes when it is not so much conviction of the desirability of virtue that is needed, as enlightenment to perceive where virtue's upward pathway lies; not so much the direction of the will which needs to be controlled, as its force and energy which need to be ever vivified and renewed. It is then that the moralist must needs welcome any influence, if such there be, which can pour into man's narrow vessel some overflowing of an infinite Power. It is then, too, that he will learn to perceive that the promise of a future existence might well be a source of potent stimulus rather than of enervating peace. For if we are to judge of the reward of virtue hereafter by the rewards which we see her achieving here, it is manifest that the only reward which always attends her is herself; that the only prize which is infallibly gained by performing one duty well is the power of performing yet another; the only recompense for an exalted self-forgetfulness is that a man forgets himself always more. Or rather, the only other reward is one whose sweetness also is scarcely realisable till it is attained; it is the love of kindred souls; but a love which recedes ever farther from the flatteries and indulgences which most men desire, and tends rather to become the intimate comradeship of spirits that strive towards the same goal.

Why then should those who would imagine an eternal reward for virtue imagine her as eternally rewarded in any other way ? And what need there be in a spiritual law like this to relax any soul's exertion, to encourage any low content ? By an unfailing physical law we know that the athlete attains through painful effort that alacrity and soundness which are the health of the body. And if there were an unfailing spiritual law by which the philosopher might attain, and ever attain increasingly, through strenuous virtue, that energy and self-devotedness which are the health of the soul, would there be anything in the one law or in the other to encourage either the physical or the spiritual voluptuary—the self-indulgence either of the banquet-hall or of the cloister ? There would be no need to test men by throwing an artificial uncertainty round the operation of such laws as these ; it would be enough if they could desire what was offered to them ; the ideal would become the probation.

To some minds reflections like these, rather than like M. Renan's, will be suggested by the story of Marcus, of his almost unmingled sadness, his almost stainless virtue. All will join, indeed, in admira-

tion for a life so free from every unworthy, every
dubious incitement to well-doing.  But on comparing this life with the lives of men for whom the
great French critic's sympathy is so much less—
such men, for instance, as St. Paul—we may surely
feel that if the universe be in reality so much
better than Marcus supposed, it would have done
him good, not harm, to have known it; that it
would have kindled his wisdom to a fervent glow,
such as the world can hardly hope to see, till, if
ever it be so, the dicta of science and the promises of
religion are at one; till saints are necessarily philosophers, and philosophers saints.  And yet, whatever inspiring secrets the future may hold, the
lover of humanity can never regret that Marcus
knew but what he knew.  Whatever winds of the
spirit may sweep over the sea of souls, the life of
Marcus will remain for ever as the normal high-
water mark of the unassisted virtue of man.  No
one has shown more simply or more completely
what man at any rate must do and be.  No one
has ever earned the right to say to himself with
a more tranquil assurance—in the words which
close the *Meditations*—"Depart thou then contented, for he that releaseth thee is content."


END OF VOL. I.

*Printed by* R. & R. CLARK, LIMITED, *Edinburgh.*

# The Eversley Series.

*Globe 8vo.   Cloth.   4s. net per volume.*

he Works of Matthew Arnold. 8 vols.
ESSAYS IN CRITICISM.  First Series.
ESSAYS IN CRITICISM.  Second Series.
EARLY AND NARRATIVE POEMS.
LYRIC AND ELEGIAC POEMS.
DRAMATIC AND LATER POEMS.
AMERICAN DISCOURSES.
LETTERS.  Edited by G. W. E.
RUSSELL.  2 Vols.

he Holy Bible. Arranged in para-
graphs, with an Introduction by J. W.
MACKAIL, M.A.  In 8 volumes. Vol. 1.
GENESIS—NUMBERS. Vol. 2. DEUTERO-
NOMY—2 SAMUEL.  Vol. 3. 1 KINGS—
ESTHER. Vol. 4. JOB—SONG OF SOLO-
MON. Vol. 5. ISAIAH—LAMENTATIONS.
Vol. 6. EZEKIEL—MALACHI. Vol. 7.
MATTHEW—JOHN.  Vol. 8. ACTS—
REVELATION.

Essays by George Brimley.  Third
Edition.

Chaucer's Canterbury Tales. Edited by
A. W. POLLARD.  2 Vols.

Miscellaneous Writings of Dean
Church. Collected Edition. 9 Vols.
MISCELLANEOUS ESSAYS.
DANTE : and other Essays.
ST. ANSELM. | SPENSER. | BACON.
THE OXFORD MOVEMENT.  Twelve
Years, 1833-1845.
THE BEGINNING OF THE MIDDLE
AGES.  (Included in this Series by
permission of Messrs. LONGMANS
& Co.)
OCCASIONAL PAPERS.  Selected from
*The Guardian, The Times,* and *The
Saturday Review,* 1846-1890. 2 Vols.

Life and Letters of Dean Church.
Edited by his Daughter, MARY C.
CHURCH.

Lectures and Essays by W. K. Clifford,
F.R.S.  Edited by LESLIE STEPHEN
and Sir F. POLLOCK.  New Edition.
2 Vols.

Collected Works of Emerson.  6 Vols.
With Introduction by JOHN MORLEY.
MISCELLANIES. | ESSAYS. | POEMS.
ENGLISH TRAITS AND REPRESENTA-
TIVE MEN.
THE CONDUCT OF LIFE, AND SOCIETY
AND SOLITUDE.
LETTERS AND SOCIAL AIMS.

Letters of Edward FitzGerald. Edited
by W. A. WRIGHT.  2 Vols.
More Letters of Edward FitzGerald.
Letters of Edward FitzGerald to
Fanny Kemble, 1871-1883. Edited by
W. A. WRIGHT.

Pausanias and other Greek Sketches.
By J. G. FRAZER, M.A.

Goethe's Maxims and Reflections.
Translated, with Introduction, by T. B.
SAUNDERS.
\*\*\* *The Scientific and Artistic
Maxims were selected by Professor
Huxley and Lord Leighton respectively.*

Collected Works of Thomas Gray in
Prose and Verse. 4 Vols. Edited by
EDMUND GOSSE. Vol. 1. Poems, Jour-
nals, and Essays. Vols. 2 and 3. Letters.
Vol. 4. Notes on Aristophanes and Plato.

Works by John Richard Green. 14 Vols.
HISTORY OF THE ENGLISH PEOPLE.
8 Vols.
THE MAKING OF ENGLAND.  With
Maps.  In 2 Vols.
THE CONQUEST OF ENGLAND.  With
Maps.  In 2 Vols.
STRAY STUDIES FROM ENGLAND AND
ITALY.
STRAY STUDIES.  Second Series.
OXFORD STUDIES.
HISTORICAL STUDIES.

Guesses at Truth.  By TWO BROTHERS.

The Choice of Books, and other Literary Pieces. By FREDERIC HARRISON.

Earthwork out of Tuscany.  Third
Edition.  By MAURICE HEWLETT.

Poems of Thomas Hood. Edited, with
Prefatory Memoir, by Canon AINGER.
In 2 Vols.  Vol. 1. SERIOUS POEMS.
Vol. 2. POEMS OF WIT AND HUMOUR.
With Vignettes and Portraits.

Collected Essays of R. H. Hutton. 6 Vols.
LITERARY ESSAYS.
ESSAYS ON SOME OF THE MODERN
GUIDES OF ENGLISH THOUGHT IN
MATTERS OF FAITH.
THEOLOGICAL ESSAYS.
CRITICISMS ON CONTEMPORARY
THOUGHT AND THINKERS. 2 Vols.
ASPECTS OF RELIGIOUS AND SCIEN-
TIFIC THOUGHT.  Selected from *The
Spectator,* and Edited by his Niece,
E. M. ROSCOE.  With Portrait.

Life and Works of Thomas Henry
Huxley. 12 Vols. Vol. 1. METHOD AND
RESULTS. Vol. 2. DARWINIANA. Vol. 3.
SCIENCE AND EDUCATION.  Vol. 4.
SCIENCE AND HEBREW TRADITION.
Vol. 5. SCIENCE AND CHRISTIAN
TRADITION. Vol. 6. HUME. With Helps
to the Study of Berkeley. Vol. 7. MAN'S
PLACE IN NATURE : and other An-
thropological Essays.  Vol. 8. DIS-
COURSES, BIOLOGICAL AND GEOLOGI-
CAL.  Vol. 9. EVOLUTION AND ETHICS,
AND OTHER ESSAYS. Vols. 10, 11, and 12.
LIFE AND LETTERS OF T. H. HUXLEY.
By LEONARD HUXLEY.

MACMILLAN AND CO., LTD., LONDON.

# The Eversley Series—*Continued.*

*Globe 8vo. Cloth. 4s. net per volume.*

French Poets and Novelists. By HENRY JAMES.

Partial Portraits. By HENRY JAMES.

Modern Greece. Two Lectures. By Sir RICHARD JEBB.

Letters of John Keats to his Family and Friends. Edited by SIDNEY COLVIN.

The Works of Charles Kingsley. 13 Vols.
WESTWARD HO! 2 Vols.
HYPATIA. 2 Vols.
YEAST. 1 Vol.
ALTON LOCKE. 2 Vols.
TWO YEARS AGO. 2 Vols.
HEREWARD THE WAKE. 2 Vols.
POEMS. 2 Vols.

The Works of Charles Lamb. Edited, with Introduction and Notes, by Canon AINGER. 6 Vols.
THE ESSAYS OF ELIA.
POEMS, PLAYS, AND MISCELLANEOUS ESSAYS.
MRS. LEICESTER'S SCHOOL, and other Writings.
TALES FROM SHAKESPEARE. By CHARLES and MARY LAMB.
THE LETTERS OF CHARLES LAMB. 2 Vols.

Life of Charles Lamb. By Canon AINGER.

Historical Essays. By J. B. LIGHTFOOT, D.D.

The Poetical Works of John Milton. Edited, with Memoir, Introduction, and Notes, by DAVID MASSON, M.A. 3 Vols.
VOL. 1. THE MINOR POEMS.
VOL. 2. PARADISE LOST.
VOL. 3. PARADISE REGAINED, AND SAMSON AGONISTES.

Collected Works of John Morley. 11 Vols.
VOLTAIRE. 1 Vol.
ROUSSEAU. 2 Vols.
DIDEROT AND THE ENCYCLOPÆDISTS. 2 Vols.
ON COMPROMISE. 1 Vol.
MISCELLANIES. 3 Vols.
BURKE. 1 Vol.
STUDIES IN LITERATURE. 1 Vol.

Essays by F. W. H. Myers. 3 Vols.
SCIENCE AND A FUTURE LIFE, AND OTHER ESSAYS.
CLASSICAL ESSAYS.
MODERN ESSAYS.

Records of Tennyson, Ruskin, and Browning. By ANNE THACKERAY RITCHIE.

The Works of Sir John R. Seeley K.C.M.G., Litt.D. 5 Vols.
THE EXPANSION OF ENGLAND. Two Courses of Lectures.
LECTURES AND ESSAYS.
ECCE HOMO. A Survey of the Life and Work of Jesus Christ.
NATURAL RELIGION.
LECTURES ON POLITICAL SCIENCE.

The Works of Shakespeare. 10 Vols. With short Introductions and Footnotes by Professor C. H. HERFORD.
Vol. 1. LOVE'S LABOUR'S LOST—COMEDY OF ERRORS—TWO GENTLEMEN OF VERONA—MIDSUMMER-NIGHT'S DREAM.
Vol. 2. TAMING OF THE SHREW—MERCHANT OF VENICE—MERRY WIVES OF WINDSOR—TWELFTH NIGHT—AS YOU LIKE IT.
Vol. 3. MUCH ADO ABOUT NOTHING—ALL'S WELL THAT ENDS WELL—MEASURE FOR MEASURE—TROILUS AND CRESSIDA.
Vol. 4. PERICLES—CYMBELINE—THE WINTER'S TALE—THE TEMPEST.
Vol. 5. HENRY VI.: First Part—HENRY VI.: Second Part—HENRY VI.: Third Part—RICHARD III.
Vol. 6. KING JOHN—RICHARD II.—HENRY IV.: First Part—HENRY IV.: Second Part.
Vol. 7. HENRY V.—HENRY VIII.—TITUS ANDRONICUS—ROMEO AND JULIET.
Vol. 8. JULIUS CÆSAR—HAMLET—OTHELLO.
Vol. 9. KING LEAR—MACBETH—ANTONY AND CLEOPATRA.
Vol. 10. CORIOLANUS—TIMON OF ATHENS—POEMS.

The Works of James Smetham.
LETTERS. With an Introductory Memoir. Edited by SARAH SMETHAM and WILLIAM DAVIES. With a Portrait.
LITERARY WORKS. Edited by WILLIAM DAVIES.

Life of Swift. By Sir HENRY CRAIK, K.C.B. 2 Vols. New Edition.

Selections from the Writings of Thoreau. Edited by H. S. SALT.

Essays in the History of Religious Thought in the West. By Bishop WESTCOTT, D.D.

The Works of William Wordsworth. Edited by Professor KNIGHT. 10 Vols.
POETICAL WORKS. 8 Vols.
PROSE WORKS. 2 Vols.
The Journals of Dorothy Wordsworth. 2 Vols.

MACMILLAN AND CO., LTD., LONDON.

# MACMILLAN'S LIBRARY

OF

# ENGLISH CLASSICS

Edited by A. W. POLLARD.

A Series of reprints of Standard Works in Library Form

*Demy 8vo. Cloth elegant. Price 3s. 6d. net per volume. Also Roxburgh Binding. Specially suitable for Presentation. Green Morocco Backs, Cloth Sides, and Gilt Tops. Price 5s. net per volume.*

MACMILLAN AND CO., Ltd., LONDON.

CPSIA information can be obtained
at www.ICGtesting.com
Printed in the USA
BVOW06*0823180917
495016BV00010B/10/P